√

Contemporary
Gothic

D0793103

Focus on Contemporary Issues (FOCI) addresses the pressing problems, ideas and debates of the new millennium. Subjects are drawn from the arts, sciences and humanities, and are linked by the impact they have had or are having on contemporary culture. FOCI books are intended for an intelligent, alert audience with a general understanding of, and curiosity about, the intellectual debates shaping culture today. Instead of easing readers into a comfortable awareness of particular fields, these books are combative. They offer points of view, take sides and are written with passion.

SERIES EDITORS
Barrie Bullen and Peter Hamilton

In the same series

Cool Rules
Dick Pountain and David Robins

Chromophobia
David Batchelor

Global Dimensions
John Rennie Short

Celebrity
Chris Rojek

Activism!
Tim Jordan

Animal
Erica Fudge

Dreamtelling
Pierre Sorlin

Anarchism
Seán M. Sheehan

The Happiness Paradox
Ziyad Marar

First Peoples
Jeffrey Sissons

Retro
Elizabeth E. Guffey

Stalking
Bran Nicol

Contemporary Gothic

CATHERINE SPOONER

REAKTION BOOKS

Published by Reaktion Books Ltd
33 Great Sutton Street
London EC1V ODX, UK

www.reaktionbooks.co.uk

First published 2006

Printed and bound in Great Britain
by Cromwell Press, Trowbridge, Wiltshire

British Library Cataloguing in Publishing Data
Spooner, Catherine, Ph. D
Contemporary Gothic. – (Focus on contemporary issues)
    1. Goth culture (Subculture) 2. Gothic revival (Literature) – Social aspects
    3. Gothic revival (Art) – Social aspects
    I. Title
    306.1

    ISBN-13: 978 1 861893 017
    ISBN-10: 1 86189 301 9

Contents

Introduction:
Reviving Gothic

While Christmas shopping in 2002, I came across a shop in my local mall temporarily devoted to nothing but calendars. Alongside the multiple images of puppies, kittens, busty babes, David Beckham, Beardsley prints and the landscapes of Provence was a calendar simply titled 'Gothic'. On closer inspection, this proved to be a compilation of fine art images dating from the Renaissance to the late nineteenth century, united in a fantastic or funereal theme. What interested me about this product was not only the fact that 'Gothic' had clearly become a concept worth marketing to a mass audience – or at least a sizeable niche within that audience – but also the choice of images that supposedly comprised 'Gothic' taste. The calendar incorporated some well-known artists (Goya, Munch, Cézanne) and some less well-known ones (Evelyn De Morgan, Louis Welden Hawkins, Henry Singleton); but few of these artists would on their own be regarded as 'Gothic' without a great deal of qualification by any self-respecting art historian. Taken together, however, this collection of graveyards, skeletons and monstrous imaginings seemed to encapsulate exactly what Gothic – for me, at least, and presumably for the target market of the calendar – is about.

In contemporary Western culture, the Gothic lurks in all sorts of unexpected corners. Like a malevolent virus, Gothic narratives have escaped the confines of literature and spread across disciplinary boundaries to infect all kinds of media, from fashion and advertising to the way contemporary events are constructed in mass culture. Goth musicians such as Nick Cave and Robert Smith of The Cure have become critically acclaimed broadsheet staples, exemplars of middle-class taste, while teenage Goths continue to preoccupy the media and even appear as regular characters on *Coronation Street*. But while we all may think that we can recognize the Gothic when we see it – we are all amateur Van Helsings, well versed in the characteristics of the vampire and its fellow creatures of the night – few of us ask questions about why Gothic is so popular at this time, or what its contemporary manifestations might mean. Those who do seek to understand contemporary Gothic tend to resort to clichés: millennial anxiety is one of the most common, in the run-up to the year 2000 and beyond; desensitization to the everyday horrors of the modern world another (this argument is at least as old as the 1790s, when it was introduced by the Marquis de Sade).[1]

There is much more to the Gothic, however, than either apocalyptic gloom or cheap thrills. Gothic texts deal with a variety of themes just as pertinent to contemporary culture as to the eighteenth and nineteenth centuries, when Gothic novels first achieved popularity: the legacies of the past and its burdens on the present; the radically provisional or divided nature of the self; the construction of peoples or individuals as monstrous or 'other'; the preoccupation with bodies that are modified, grotesque or diseased. Gothic has become so pervasive precisely because it is so apposite to the representation of contemporary concerns. While we should perhaps be careful of assuming that Gothic simply reflects social anxieties in a straightforward manner – as a genre deliberately intended to provoke horror and unease, it plays to audience expectations and therefore is rather too self-conscious to illuminate our most secret fears – it certainly engages with them on a variety of often quite sophisticated levels. It provides a

Contemporary Gothic icon Nick Cave, 1993.

language and a lexicon through which anxieties both personal and collective can be narrativized.

Faced with the bewildering range of contemporary manifestations of the Gothic, it is important to know where Gothic has come from: Gothic did not emerge ready-made and ripe for exploitation into the modern era, it has a history, over which it has changed, developed and accrued multiple layers of meaning. Gothic as a genre is profoundly concerned with the past, conveyed through both historical settings and narrative interruptions of the past into the present; for Victor Sage and Allan Lloyd-Smith it provides

Paul Cézanne, *Skull and Candlestick*, 1866, oil on canvas (detail).

'the perfect anonymous language for the peculiar unwillingness of the past to go away'.[2] It is also, however, profoundly concerned with its own past, self-referentially dependent on traces of other stories, familiar images and narrative structures, intertextual allusions. If this could be said to be true of a great many kinds of literature or film, then Gothic has a greater degree of self-consciousness about its nature, cannibalistically consuming the dead body of its own tradition.

Fittingly, considering the genre's preoccupation with all kinds of revenants and returns from the dead, Gothic has throughout its history taken the form of a series of revivals: the period of medieval architecture to which the eighteenth- and nineteenth-century Gothic Revivalists harked back, for example, was no more 'original' than they were themselves, being named after a northern European tribal people of the Dark Ages. There is no 'original' Gothic; it is always already a revival of something else. Indeed,

Evelyn De Morgan, *The Angel of Death*, 1890, oil on canvas (detail). The Cézanne and the De Morgan are stylistic juxtapositions on a 2003 Gothic calendar.

the Gothic's dependence on the concept of revival may provide a means by which we can understand Gothic in its myriad contemporary forms, some of which seem a long way from the genteel spectres and highly strung heroines of late eighteenth-century fiction, never mind the Gothic cathedrals of the Middle Ages.

To revive is to assume fresh life (or indeed, to *give* fresh life). As frequent readers of Gothic fiction will know, such returns from the dead are staple features of Gothic narrative; but like Frankenstein's monster, these revivals seldom take exactly the same shape they possessed before. The notion of revival can be seen to imply a reappropriation and reinvention of previous forms rather than a straightforward repetition. Thus contemporary Gothic discourses can be viewed as relating to an earlier Gothic tradition while expressing at times an entirely different range of cultural agendas. My Gothic calendar (which I duly bought and hung in my study) provides an excellent example: reordered and placed in a new context, these images are reanimated with a new identity. Defined through subject matter rather than style or historical movement, Cézanne's avant-garde, Post-Impressionist *Skull and Candlestick* can sit happily next to Evelyn De Morgan's conservative, late Pre-Raphaelite *Angel of Death* without apparent contradiction. The process of plundering the past for artefacts that will anachronistically express a current taste is analogous to the eighteenth-century Gothic novelist Ann Radcliffe's liberal quotation from Shakespeare and Milton, or Horace Walpole's collection of medieval curios to furnish what a rival disparagingly called his 'Gothic mousetrap', Strawberry Hill. This Gothic revival, however, is presented pre-packaged, niche-marketed, its meanings over-determined. There is, moreover, something paradoxical about the very form of a Gothic calendar: if Gothic is inherently concerned with the incursions of the past into the present, with hauntings and repetition, it sits oddly with the sequential tabulation of calendar time, which always points not towards what has already happened in the past, but to what is about to happen in the future (to be truly Gothic, my calendar should be rediscovered many years after my death, covered in illegible symbols and indecipherable in several places due to mould and the gnawing of rodents).

Goths, Gothick, Gothic

The word 'Gothic' has a long usage, beginning with the northern European peoples who sacked Rome in the fifth century AD. Although in their way a sophisticated culture, possessing superior skills of horsemanship, the

Goths' nomadic, tribal existence led them to be presented by subsequent generations as barbarians, primitive peoples who with brute force had overturned the cultural achievements of Roman civilization. This enabled the construction of a convenient set of dualisms, primitive versus civilized, barbarism versus culture, which has structured the way the term has been understood throughout its history. While anyone using the word 'Gothic' in the present day is unlikely to be referring to the fifth-century Goths, this nomadic people's violent overthrow of what is conventionally viewed in the West as one of the greatest civilizations of all time lies behind the modern understanding of Gothic as the passionate overthrow of reason.

The term 'Gothic' re-emerged in the seventeenth century, in Britain as a means of retrospectively describing a style of medieval ecclesiastical architecture, one that ignored the clean lines and curves of Classical styles and instead embellished its constructions with pointed arches, grotesque angles and excrescences, gargoyles, stiff elongated figures and elaborate detail. The soaring spires and naves of buildings such as Chartres Cathedral and York Minster inspired spiritual uplift, architecturally implying the glory of God to the worshippers within. Like the Goths themselves, the Gothic style was most characteristic of northern Europe, expressive of a particular cultural sensibility distinct from the more Classically derived or Byzantine aesthetic of the Mediterranean countries. It was also, in a sense, the first Gothic revival, in that its overthrow of Classicism with its wild, fantastic shapes echoed that earlier overthrow of Roman civilization with barbarism by the Goths.

Although Gothic architecture fell out of style during the Renaissance, the term 'Gothick' took on new significance for the antiquarians of the late seventeenth and eighteenth centuries. For these men, 'Gothick' could be appropriated as representing a specifically British cultural tradition – a tradition of political freedom and progressivism embodied in the achievements of the Middle Ages. The anti-Classical associations of Gothic were reinterpreted as a source of pride; they represented the indigenous identity of Britain that had resisted Roman colonization. Country houses that revived the medieval Gothic style were the outcome of this reappraisal, as the landed elite sought to invest their estates with its ideological significance. Gothic was secularized and imbued with Whiggish politics.

The emergence of the Gothic novel in the second half of the eighteenth century, however, skewed the ideological significance of Gothic once again. Over the course of the next hundred years two quite distinct sets of meanings attached to Gothic began to develop. On the one hand, Gothic represented a mythical medieval Britain, where chivalry held sway, social order prevailed and religious belief was unchallenged. On the other, it represented a time of barbarity and feudalism before the blessed arrival of the Enlightenment and the benefits of science and reason that it bestowed. These two separate urges were politicized: reactionary and progressive, Tory and Whig, nostalgic and proto-modernist. They resulted in two very different forms of art: on the one hand, the Gothic Revivalism of eighteenth- and nineteenth-century architecture and painting; on the other, the sensational narratives of the Gothic novel. These two strands are sometimes (understandably) confused, because of their shared name and fascination with the Middle Ages. However, while novels like Matthew Lewis's *The Monk* (1796) portrayed medieval Spain as riddled with Catholic hypocrisy, terrorized by the Inquisition and easy prey for Satan, Augustus Welby Pugin's Houses of Parliament (1835–68) evoked the Middle Ages as a time of spiritual purity and social cohesion, before the ravages of industrialization, when Britain had produced its greatest architectural achievements, its Gothic cathedrals. Gothic, then, is inherently split: as Chris Baldick has suggested, 'the most troublesome aspect of the term "Gothic" is, indeed, that literary Gothic is really anti-Gothic'.[3]

The most distinctive feature of Gothic architecture is its upward line – the pointed arch aspiring towards heaven. For nineteenth-century Revivalists, it was a transcendently spiritual style, a style that could be invested with faith as well as politics. Thus Pugin sought to emulate the

Atmospheric ruins: medieval Gothic architecture, Gothic Revival sensibility. Louis Daguerre's oil painting *Ruins of Holyrood Chapel* (1825).

arches and spires of Salisbury, Lincoln and York in contemporary architecture, while the German Nazarenes and British Pre-Raphaelites attempted to return to the purity of style of the medieval painters, and William Morris restored the values of craftsmanship to interior design. While the Victorian Gothic Revival may have provided plenty of useful locations for contemporary Gothic film and fashion shoots, therefore, it is only tangentially related to what David Punter has called 'the literature of terror'.[4] Ruskin and Pugin did not want to enjoy vicariously the tyrannies of the past, but to escape the grotesqueries of the industrial present. Interestingly, one of the main markets for Gothic Revival painting and architecture was among

Douglas Gordon, *Monster*, 1996–7, colour photo in a painted wood frame.

the newly rich industrialists, suggesting that despite its glorious visions of the past, the Gothic Revival was a distinctly modern way of viewing the world.

Contemporary art, however, has returned not to the art of the Gothic Revival but to the alternative tradition of the Gothic novel for inspiration. Contemporary artists working in what could be described as a Gothic idiom, including Cindy Sherman, Rachel Whiteread, Douglas Gordon, Jake and Dinos Chapman, Jane and Louise Wilson, and Gregory Crewdson, are concerned not with spiritual transcendence and historical nostalgia, but with the themes of haunting and imprisonment found in the Gothic novel. Cindy Sherman's photographs of dolls and medical mannequins in monstrous scenarios, as well as her grotesque re-creation of faux-historical portraits with masks and fake body parts, play on the characteristic Gothic tension between bodily disgust and its displacement into surface 'trappings'. Rachel Whiteread's *House* (1993), a full-sized plaster-cast of the interior of a condemned Victorian terrace, evoked a structure imbued with the history of its inhabitants, as well as a sense of its own passing. Douglas Gordon deliberately evokes seminal Gothic texts by Robert Louis Stevenson and James Hogg in his sound and video installations, amplifying a significantly Scottish Gothic preoccupation with duality and the shattered psyche. Jane and Louise Wilson's eerie videos of empty military-industrial spaces evoke the ghosts of the Cold War. Their video installation of an empty House of Commons, tracing the symbols and spaces of political power, tellingly marries Pugin's Gothic architectural idealism with the darker sensibility of the Gothic literary and cinematic tradition. Similarly, Cathy de Monchaux's sumptuously crafted sculptures take the decorative forms of Gothic architecture and merge them with the visceral shapes and textures of the human body, suggestively evoking a range of secret, potentially cruel desires.

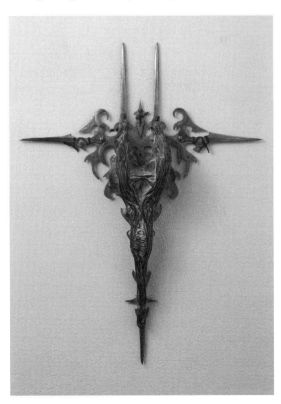

Cathy de Monchaux, *Worried About the Weather?*, 1995, brass, copper, leather and chalk.

Defining Gothic

As yet, the most satisfactory definition of literary Gothic appears in Chris Baldick's 'Introduction' to *The Oxford Book of Gothic Tales*. According to Baldick, a Gothic text should comprise 'a fearful sense of inheritance in time with a claustrophobic sense of enclosure in space, these two dimensions reinforcing one another to produce an impression of sickening descent into disintegration'.[5] In Gothic texts, the past returns with sickening force: the dead rise from the grave or lay their cold hands upon the shoulders of the living. This fearful scenario is compounded by physical imprisonment: the labyrinthine underground vaults and torture chambers of eighteenth-century Gothic texts; the secret passages and attics riddling the ancestral mansions of the nineteenth century; the chambers of the human heart and brain in twentieth-century writing. As Emily Dickinson, a poet with a frequently Gothic awareness, wrote, 'One need not be a chamber – to be haunted': in twentieth-century film and fiction, the troubling ghosts of past traumas were not restricted to architectural locales, but made the mind itself a kind of prison.[6] Thus Toni Morrison's novel *Beloved* (1988) presents its freed and escaped slaves as liberated from physical bondage but still imprisoned by their psychological scars, while, as several critics have noted, one of the favourite tropes of contemporary Gothic is the repressed memory of childhood abuse, as in Stephen King's *The Shining* (1977). Just as Edgar Allen Poe's House of Usher ultimately crumbles into the tarn at its foot, so these psychological prisons characteristically disintegrate under repeated mental strain, terminating in madness and breakdown.

In Gothic texts, therefore, the past is a site of terror, of an injustice that must be resolved, an evil that must be exorcised. It is not, as in the architecture of the Gothic Revival, invested with nostalgia or idealism. The past chokes the present, prevents progress and the march towards personal or social enlightenment. In Bram Stoker's *Dracula* (1897) the vampire's ancient aristocratic bloodline/bloodlust threatens the ruthlessly modern young people who seek to foil his evil plans with the aid of their typewriters, phonographs, train timetables and bang-up-to-date criminological theory. On the other hand, the distancing technique of many Gothic texts (most of the early novels are set on what Robert Miles has labelled 'the Gothic cusp' between the Middle Ages and the beginnings of the Enlightenment, while those written today are frequently located in the Victorian era) suggests that we can relegate these terrors to the past, indulge our passion for pleasurable tyrannies while safe in the knowledge of our present enlightenment.[7] As Chris Baldick and Robert Mighall suggest in an influential essay on 'Gothic Criticism', Gothic is an eminently bourgeois form, and its values for the most part 'tamely humanitarian'.[8] They insist that 'There are good practical reasons why the middle class should sleep more soundly than other social groups can, and there is no evidence that it sleeps less soundly after curling up with a titillating anthology of vampire stories.'[9] Perhaps it is only secure cultures that produce Gothic texts, hence the relative dearth of European Gothic in the period of political and economic instability between the First World War and the early 1960s.

The desire to fictionalize the past in Gothic terms can be identified in all sorts of situations, which might not otherwise seem to have anything to do with Gothic. In 2003, for example, I visited the Royal Academy's highly acclaimed *Aztecs* exhibition in London, which brought together for the first time hundreds of artefacts from the fourteenth- to sixteenth-century Central American civilization. In modern Western terms the Aztec culture was bloodthirsty and violent, involving human sacrifice and a variety of other gruesome rituals. Much of its artwork seems macabre to contemporary viewers, featuring flayed or mutilated human bodies or graphic representations of grisly legends. As I wandered around the crowded galleries (this was an overwhelmingly popular exhibition), I overheard several conversations expressing shock and disgust at the cruelty of Aztec culture. One woman even suggested that it was a blessing the Spaniards had wiped them out, a view echoed in broadsheet reviews and by television pundits.

Sixteenth-century Spain, however, boasted the Inquisition, witch-hunts, bullfighting and horrific public executions. It was, of course, precisely the material of eighteenth-century Gothic, the salacious setting for novels like Lewis's *The Monk*. For Lewis, the cruelties of Catholicism provided the titillating background to a variety of horrific practices: not only the protagonist's rape, matricide, incest, Satanic pact, suggestive necrophilia and impressively gory death, but also institutionalized cruelties such as the forced entrance of young women into convents and the torture and incarceration of those who subsequently broke their vows. While these were undoubtedly sensational fantasies on Lewis's part, rather than reflective of any historical reality, the way in which Lewis and his Protestant readers constructed the late medieval, Catholic Spanish as a detestable other, through which their own modernity and enlightenment could be verified, bears no small resemblance to the twenty-first century response to the Aztecs. Although neither the Aztecs nor their art are Gothic in themselves – they belong to an entirely different system of representation – viewers of the exhibition made them Gothic: a past horror that raises a gleeful shudder even as we congratulate ourselves on the collective progress of humanity. On the eve of the bloody and unpopular war with Iraq (another implicitly barbaric regime), this psychological distancing of horror into a fantasized historical narrative seemed particularly defensive, the realities of civilian casualties, suicide bombers and media manipulation in fact potentially far less 'civilized' than the Aztecs' heavily ritualized warfare and richly symbolic sacrifices. Meanwhile, the notion that barbaric cultures deserve to be colonized and 'civilized' by others served to underline the self-justification of the British and American governments' war policy. Gothic here seemed to perform a particular kind of cultural work, a means through which Western culture could displace its fears into an exotic, distanced other and thus feel safe.

Fin-de-millennium, fin d'innocence

What was interesting about my experience of *Aztecs* was that it seemed a vivid illustration of what a number of critics, including Mark Edmundson in *Nightmare on Main Street*, have begun to identify as 'Gothic culture'.[10] Recent research on the Gothic has started to identify characteristically Gothic narrative patterns working themselves free of the texts in which we are most accustomed to recognize them and replicating themselves across culture. While we should be careful of applying the term Gothic without discrimination – such criticism runs the risk of being reductive – it is certainly true that in the last few decades of the twentieth century and at the beginning of the twenty-first, Gothic narratives began to achieve increasing prominence in both popular and academic culture. As Angela Carter commented in 1974, in the afterword to her collection of darkly erotic short stories, *Fireworks*, 'We live in Gothic times.'[11] Her earlier novel *Love* (1971), its title ironically evoking 1960s hippy idealism, specifically attempted to capture the Gothic zeitgeist as it dissected the dark aftermath of the Sixties, its art-school anti-heroine Annabel descending into madness and suicide as the dream of free expression turns sour.

As suggested above, the preoccupation with the darker side of human life – death, crime, insanity, perversion, obsessive desire, the supernatural and the occult – has sometimes been labelled a *fin-de-siècle* phenomenon, an apocalyptic tendency that inevitably climaxes at the *fin-de-millennium*. Critics note the apparent clusters of Gothic activity – novels, art, cultural decadence – that accompanied the 1790s, 1890s and, ultimately, the 1990s. David Punter, for example, suggests that Gothic has 'something quite specific to do with the turn of centuries, as though the very attempt to turn over a new leaf unavoidably involves conjuring the shadow of the past'.[12] In the aftermath of the French Revolution, according to the Marquis de Sade, a jaded audience sought titillation from the supernatural in fiction by Ann Radcliffe and Matthew Lewis: 'In four or five years, there was not an individual left who had not felt misfortunes and who, in a century famous for its writing, was not able to depict them. In order therefore to confer some interest on their productions, it was necessary to appeal to hell for aid.'[13] At the end of the nineteenth century, the 'sexual anarchy' identified by the critic Elaine Showalter led to a preoccupation with the darker side of human desire: the night-time perambulations of Dracula, Dorian Gray and Dr Jekyll's alter ego, the 'troglodytic' Mr Hyde.[14] As the Millennium approached, Christoph Grunenberg, among many others, linked the resurgence of interest in Gothic to the peculiar nature of the times: 'The current Gothic mood, as much as it has become a commercially exploited fashion and entertainment phenomenon, is symptomatic of a continuing spiritual emptiness at the end of the century.'[15]

Nevertheless, our culture's preoccupation with the Gothic cannot be wholly attributed to millennial anxiety. To begin with, the pattern by which Gothic texts apparently appear in greater numbers towards the end of each century has to a large degree been exaggerated. Many Gothic texts do not fit this pattern: in the twentieth century, for example, Daphne du Maurier's *Rebecca* (1938) and the great horror films produced by German Expressionism in the 1920s and Hollywood's Universal Studios in the 1930s and '40s. In the nineteenth century, the works of the Brontës and Edgar Allan Poe also defied this pattern, while two of the most influential Gothic novels ever written, Mary Shelley's *Frankenstein* and Charles Maturin's *Melmoth, the Wanderer*, appeared in 1818 and 1820 respectively. The passion for Gothic shows no sign of abating, either, now that the Millennium has passed; the fashion pages continue to herald 'the return of Gothic', while Gothic artefacts of the new century so far include Sarah Waters's best-selling novel *Fingersmith* (2002) and the big-budget vampire films *Blade II*

(2002), *Blade Trinity* (2004), *Underworld* (2004) and *Van Helsing* (2004). At the end of the twentieth century, the level of media hype surrounding the Millennium and what might possibly happen at it (the speculated effects of the Millennium Bug, mass suicide pacts among millennial cults) ensured that there was a mass appetite for the enjoyably doomy: films like *End of Days* (1999), featuring Arnold Schwarzenegger battling his ultimate adversary in the form of an apocalypse-hungry Satan, were a big box-office draw, but seemed to elaborate on media hype rather than genuine anxiety.

What distinguishes contemporary Gothic, the Gothic texts of the late twentieth and early twenty-first centuries, is on the whole not a sense of impending apocalypse, but rather three quite independent factors. Contemporary Gothic possesses a new self-consciousness about its own nature; it has reached new levels of mass production, distribution and audience awareness, enabled by global consumer culture; and it has crossed disciplinary boundaries to be absorbed into all forms of media. Contemporary Gothic is not preoccupied with the end of the world, but rather the end of innocence. Gothic has from the beginning been a very knowing and self-aware genre – it was artificially constructed by a camp antiquarian, Horace Walpole, and parodies appeared almost as soon as the first novels – but post-Freud, Marx and feminism, it has gained a sexual and political self-consciousness unavailable to the earliest Gothic novelists. More than two centuries of Gothic revivals have also enabled layers of irony beyond anything that Horace Walpole could have imagined, so that his *The Castle of Otranto* (1764) now seems endearingly clumsy to modern readers. Gothic has now, furthermore, become supremely commercialized, be it mainstream or niche-marketed. Gothic no longer crops up only in film and fiction, but also fashion, furniture, computer games, youth culture, advertising. Gothic has always had mass appeal, but in today's economic climate it is big business. Above all, Gothic sells.

This is not a particularly new development. Gothic has always been closely allied to consumer culture. As E. J. Clery has explained, the rise of

Gothic fiction was intimately related to the Enlightenment, since it is only a society that has stopped seriously believing in ghosts that is able to turn them into the stuff of entertainment. Nevertheless, since thrilling tales of spectres and superstition failed to fulfil the Enlightenment demand that literature be instructive, supernatural fiction became the ultimate luxury product, conceived purely in terms of excess.[16] So far as the literary marketplace was concerned, Gothic fiction was enormously successful: in the 1790s Ann Radcliffe commanded what were then considered enormous advances for her novels, while Matthew Lewis's *The Monk* was a *succès de scandale* that ran into five editions in the four years following its publication. In the 1860s *The Woman in White*, Wilkie Collins's Victorian update of the Radcliffean romance, spawned a mass of tie-in merchandise from waltzes to bonnets. George Du Maurier's *Trilby* (1894), with its Gothicized villain Svengali, was by some estimates the bestselling novel of the nineteenth century, and again was linked to a variety of merchandise and events including Trilby shoes, sweets, soaps, sausages, concerts, parties and, of course, the celebrated Trilby hat. Much of the early criticism of Gothic romance and its successors, such as the Newgate and Sensation novels, was precisely of its popularity: its avid consumption by middle-class misses, or later in the nineteenth century by servants and shop-girls, led to its condemnation for spreading moral laxity and nervous over-excitement. From its inception, there has been a kind of critical snobbishness against Gothic, springing from the cultural elitism that decries any form of mass entertainment. In the late twentieth century, however, a critical preoccupation with the marginal and the transgressive led to an inversion of that elitism: now Gothic is all the rage because it can ostensibly be used as a tool of subversion against the cultural elite. Gothic has apparently become popular among academics because it is invested with the thrill of the forbidden, which in this context is not entirely different from the thrill of the low-brow. Suddenly, Gothic is PC: championed by feminists and queer theorists for its level of attention to women and non-heteronormative sexualities; the reading material of the masses; the space in which the burdens of colonial guilt could be explored and exorcised. Gothic has become an idealized space for textual disruption; yet again, it is the means through which we reify our own enlightenment.

The academic passion for Gothic is reflected by its widespread favour throughout mainstream popular culture. This may seem like a paradox: in a culture devoted to the pursuit of happiness, where racial unity and equality have become fashion statements used to market soft drinks and leisure clothing, how can a genre with associations of evil, death and decay, sensory disorientation and psychological instability, be regarded as anything other than a minority taste, either avant-garde subversion or cult underground predilection? This is how many contemporary critics would like to see Gothic: as a marginal genre, invested with subversive potential; a form in which the dark unconscious desires of our pleasure-seeking society are exposed and dissected. Yet Stephen King, writer of popular horror novels, is America's bestselling author; the vampire chronicler Anne Rice is not far behind. The self-styled 'Antichrist Superstar' Marilyn Manson has sold millions of copies of his Gothic-influenced albums across the world, while the neo-Goth band Evanescence spent four weeks at the top of the British charts in the summer of 2003. Gothic images are used on television to sell everything from Smirnoff vodka to Ariel washing-powder. Films like *A Nightmare on Elm Street* (1984), *Silence of the Lambs* (1990), *Bram Stoker's Dracula* (1992), *Interview With the Vampire* (1994) and *Scream* (1996) are huge box-office hits, their sinister villains – Freddie Krueger, Hannibal Lecter, Lestat – becoming playground anti-heroes. One of the most popular television series of the turn of the century was *Buffy the Vampire Slayer*, which, along with its spin-off *Angel* and similar series like *Sabrina the Teenage Witch* and *Charmed*, seemed to indicate a new interest in the dark side among teenagers, whether disaffected or otherwise. By the turn of the twentieth century, Gothic had consolidated its position as the material of mainstream entertainment.

Gothic Transformations

In what other ways can the contemporary Gothic revival be said to relate to those of the eighteenth and nineteenth centuries? Inevitably, the form has changed over the course of the last 200 years. It has spawned other genres, like science fiction and the detective novel; it has interacted with literary movements, social pressures and historical conditions to become a more diverse, loosely defined set of narrative conventions and literary tropes. Alastair Fowler suggests that literary Gothic began as a distinct 'kind' of fixed genre, 'the gothic romance', but that this initial form 'yielded a gothic mode that outlasted it', or, in other words, a more flexible means of description that does not present a definitive statement about its object, but can be applied to a variety of different kinds of texts: 'the maritime adventure (*The Narrative of Arthur Gordon Pym*), the psychological novel (*Titus Groan*), the crime novel (*Edwin Drood*), the short story, the film script' and so on.[17] A text may be Gothic and simultaneously many other things. *The X-Files*, for example, is a detective series in the Gothic mode, but is also science fiction, conspiracy theory and a buddy cop drama. It is worth raising Jacques Derrida's question whether texts ever 'belong' to any one genre: rather, he argues, they 'participate' in genres.[18] To participate does not entail complete identification; it merely suggests a relationship with that genre.

Thus Gothic motifs, narrative structures or images may arise in a variety of contexts – from pop music to advertising – that may not otherwise seem Gothic in any straightforward sense. Nevertheless, these themes and motifs deliberately recall the Gothic and implicitly engage in dialogue with the form as it emerged in the eighteenth century. They may subtly alter the Gothic as it is traditionally understood, appropriate it for ends perhaps entirely different from, or even contrary to, those of its earliest practitioners, even 'de-Gothicize' conventional images, such as those of Frankenstein's monster or Dracula's castle, by draining them of their power to induce horror or the sublime. Despite these alterations, however, these images and narratives only achieve meaning through evoking Gothic in the first place. A good example would be the children's toys that fill the shops around Hallowe'en. Most of these plastic jack-o'-lanterns, glow-in-the-dark ghosts and cuddly creatures of the night are mass-produced and altogether fail to terrify: if they raise an emotion at all, it is likely to be laughter. They are domesticated, comic, trivial – props for children's play-acting. Yet there is also something deeply ironic about a rubber bat that links it irrevocably with the fiction of Radcliffe and Lewis. There is a salient tension between an object supposed to evoke fear and the cheapness and familiarity of its materials. Within Gothic fiction, props and accessories have always had a tendency to take over the narrative: as Eve Sedgwick has argued, the 'trivial' surfaces of Gothic texts so frequently dismissed by critics are in actual fact precisely where some of the most interesting Gothic effects are to be found.[19] For Sedgwick, Gothic is about the denial of depth and the insistence on the surface – on the mask rather than the face, the veil rather than what lies beneath, the disguise rather than what is disguised. The gloriously camp theatricality of Horace Walpole's *The Castle of Otranto*, with its stage villainy, moving portraits, weeping statues and supernatural suits of giant armour is replicated in the jolly commercial opportunity that is contemporary Hallowe'en.

This emphasis on surface, spectacle and performance might seem, again, supremely appropriate to contemporary culture; specifically, to the culture of postmodernity. As Allan Lloyd-Smith has pointed out, 'There are some striking parallels between the features identified in discourses concerning postmodernism and those which are focused on the Gothic tradition', one of which is precisely the foregrounding of 'an aesthetics of the surface, dominated by the depthless image'.[20] Yet while this is undoubtedly the case, there also seems to be a counteractive pull towards interiority in much contemporary Gothic. If Gothic in its eighteenth- and early nineteenth-century phase has been seen by some as a 'dark side' to Romanticism, the space where Romanticism's darker urges could be indulged, its repressions divulged, then in the twenty-first century Romanticism seems to have become a kind of shadow double to the Gothic. The desire for plenitude, for interiority and depth, found in many strands of Romanticism, haunts many contemporary Gothic texts. Jane Campion's film *The Piano* (1992), for example, plays off an erotics of costume against its mute heroine's search for self. Similarly, an album like The Cure's *Faith* (1981) combines gut-wrenching existential angst with a heightened sense of performance, replicating a more general tension within Goth subculture between performative identities expressed through costume and the quest for authentic (and sometimes anguished) self-expression. Rather than seeing Gothic or Romanticism as subsidiary to the other, it makes more sense to regard them as twin impulses, often proceeding from the same set of ideas or coexisting within the same texts. Gothic is a set of pressures acting on or within certain Romantic texts, while the demands for plenitude and self-realization associated with some strands of Romanticism continually erupt within Gothic.

Contemporary Gothic

The following chapters will attempt to offer several lines of enquiry into contemporary Gothic, suggesting some of its most salient characteristics. 'Mock Gothic' suggests that Gothic has always been about fakes – especially fake history. Horace Walpole's Strawberry Hill was a fake Gothic castle with fireplaces modelled on ancient tombs in Westminster Abbey; his Gothic tale *The Castle of Otranto* purported to be a medieval manuscript. This preoccupation with the fake spreads across contemporary culture, expressed most effectively in Baudrillard's theorization of simulacra. Texts like *The Blair Witch Project* (1998) and Mark Z. Danielewski's

House of Leaves (2000) question the nature of the forgery and the fragment, and the processes of interpretation that readers impose upon them. The vampire as simulation is addressed in Michael Almereyda's film *Nadja* (1994), as well as the reconfiguration of Gothic spaces in the postmodern context.

'Grotesque Bodies' will examine physical manifestations of Gothic, from the circus freak to the stigmatic. Forms of contemporary cultural production demonstrate a marked preoccupation with the grotesque, the abject and the artificially augmented. These range from the affectless corpses of Gunther von Hagens through the re-visitation of the carnivalesque in Katherine Dunn's *Geek Love* (1983), to a return to spirituality in the photography of Joel-Peter Witkin. The fascination with freakishness is partly based in performative notions of identity – remaking the self as monstrous – and partly in an apparently contradictory attempt to reinstate the physicality of the body in an increasingly decorporealized information society.

'Teen Demons' examines Gothic as the teenage genre of choice, an antidote to anodyne boy bands and pre-manufactured girl power. In the new Teen Gothic of texts like *Buffy the Vampire Slayer* (1997–2003) and *Ginger Snaps* (2000), teenagers are more likely to be the demons than the victims. A highly Goth-literate audience knows the horror conventions and allows them to be subjected to new ironies, with films like the *Scream* series and *The Faculty* (1998) playing with the conventions of both slasher flicks and teen movies. In the process, the role of the outsider is rewritten to appeal to an audience who buys into alienation en masse and elevates the geek to chic. This leads into the final chapter, 'Gothic Shopping', which explores the imbrications of Gothic with contemporary consumer culture. As George Romero's horror film *Dawn of the Dead* (1978) might suggest, with its endlessly proliferating zombies cruising mindlessly around a deserted shopping mall to the strains of piped muzak, there is perhaps something inherently Gothic in the replication required by mass-marketing. This chapter examines Gothic in advertising, fashion and merchandising. Taking as its argument the statement that 'Gothic sells', it attempts to delineate exactly how Gothic discourses are redeployed by those of Western consumerism.

Finally, this book seeks to discover a complex way of reading contemporary Gothic as more than just the sum of our repressed anxieties. In his Oscar-winning documentary *Bowling For Columbine* (2002) the American writer and film-maker Michael Moore suggests that contemporary America constitutes a culture of fear: citizens are continually bombarded with news bulletins warning them of imminent threats to personal and national safety even as the government pursues aggressively imperialist policies overseas. America, of course, has an incalculable influence on the other countries of the Western world through the ubiquity of its cultural products. But rather than suggest, as the critic Mark Edmundson does, for example, that Gothic is a response to this 'culture of fear', we could argue that Gothic literary and cinematic narratives, which are intrinsically concerned with the production of pleasurable fear, are appropriated by other kinds of discourses in order to produce similar (not always so pleasurable) effects. Gothic provides a language and a set of discourses with which we can talk about fear and anxiety, rather than being reducible to whatever fear happens to be promoted by the media at any given time. This book will attempt to map out a few of the ways in which this language, or set of discourses, operates in our contemporary culture.

CHAPTER ONE

Mock Gothic

Faking It

The Eerie Pub Co. is a London-based chain of Gothic theme pubs and bars, all of which sport splendidly exaggerated Gothic styling, complete with gargoyles, bubbling test tubes and doors hidden behind fake bookshelves. One can order cocktails themed around the Seven Deadly Sins or chips on coffin-shaped plates, and pre-recorded hollow laughter rings through the toilets. Due to the location of the pubs in the West End, the clientele consists mainly of tourists and office workers, although occasionally Goths and vampire fans can be spotted mingling with the suits. Some of the pubs, such as Ben Crouch's Tavern off Oxford Circus, have a tenuous relationship with the more sinister side of local history; others, like the Marlborough Head in Marble Arch, are pure decor.

Eerie Pubs can be viewed as part of a trend for stylized leisure that also encompasses Irish theme pubs, and recalls the themed bars found in Las Vegas or Disneyland. One does not really experience the Gothic in these pubs, any more than an Irish theme pub provides the experience of really being in Ireland: one may glut oneself on Gluttony or jump at the crash of thunder when opening the toilet door, but the ultimate effect is one of tongue-in-cheek jollity, and the activities that go on are no different from those taking place in countless other pubs up and down the country. Nevertheless, Eerie Pubs bear a very different relationship with their theme than do, say, Irish pubs. Ireland is, quite obviously, a real place whose inhabitants have a distinct cultural identity invested with social and political significance. Irish theme pubs offer an airbrushed version of that cultural identity, based in stereotyped signs and symbols of Irishness that lack the apparent authenticity of actually being in a genuine pub in Ireland. While it is possible, if perhaps controversial, to question such constructions of 'authentic' identity, it is difficult to deny that a having a pint in a themed Irish bar in Slough offers somewhat less than the full experience of drinking Guinness in Galway.

Gothic, on the other hand, possesses no original. As I argued in the Introduction, Gothic takes the form of a series of revivals, each based on a fantasized idea of the previous one. As a form it has always been about fakery. Horace Walpole's *The Castle of Otranto* (1764), often cited as the first Gothic novel, was supposed to be a medieval manuscript, newly discovered and translated by the author. His Twickenham mansion, Strawberry Hill, said to be the inspiration for *Otranto*, was a fake Gothic castle, its elaborate interiors copied from pictures in books and constructed in parts from papier mâché. Jerrold Hogle has argued that the 'counterfeit', or indeed 'the ghost of the counterfeit', is integral to the Gothic: the copies of the medieval found in the earliest Gothic texts did not imitate the 'original' Middle Ages but rather Renaissance representations of the Middle Ages. As he explains:

> Hence, throughout the 'Gothic revival' in the eighteenth century, the remnant of 'obligatory' or 'natural' meaning is replaced as the sign's point of reference by counterfeits *of* that remnant: portraits or armour hung on walls, painted landscapes (the 'picturesque') rather than eyewitness viewings, illustrations of the medieval

Strawberry Hill, Twickenham, in an 18th-century print.

'Gothic' in books, performances or editions of Shakespeare's plays, falsely 'authentic' reproductions (from sham Gothic 'ruins' on estates to James Macpherson's 'Ossian' poems), or pieces broken off archaic structures and reassembled quite differently, particularly at Walpole's Strawberry Hill . . . The neo-Gothic is therefore haunted by the ghost of that already spectral past and hence by its refaking of what is already fake and already an emblem of the nearly empty and dead.[1]

Thus, for Hogle, the 'ghost of the counterfeit' mediates between nostalgia for past ideologies and the freeing up or emptying out of symbols of that past for cultural exchange and profit within a capitalist system of commodities. With the shift into industrial and post-industrial modes of production, the process of the ghosting of the counterfeit also shifts along the lines laid out by Jean Baudrillard, through industrial production to simulation, leading to 'a hyperreality of signs referring to other signs that cannot root itself even in quasi-industrial moulds'.[2] Hogle notes an early example of this process in Bram Stoker's *Dracula* (1897), in which the vampire

> so attempts to consume English life before leaving Transylvania, by reading numerous documents from the 'London Directory' to 'the Law List', that he sets himself up both for turning the English people he penetrates into 'un-dead' evacuated images of their former selves and for being gradually 'read' and evacuated himself in 'the mass of material of which the record [of him] is composed', at the base of which 'there is hardly one authentic document; nothing but a mass of typewriting' that turns out to be as vampiric as its subject.[3]

Allan Lloyd-Smith elaborates on this thesis: he suggests that in contemporary Gothic texts the counterfeit, there from the beginning, is mingled with postmodern pastiche to achieve a peculiar emptiness, 'a *ghosting* of the original Gothic'.[4] Eerie Pubs, with their Gothic paraphernalia borrowed from cheap horror movie clichés, represent a ghost of the ghost of the counterfeit. As Lloyd-Smith suggests, 'The Gothic heritage becomes *Heritage Gothic*, a use of now conventional tropes that is legitimized simply through previous practice.'[5]

For E. J. Clery, Walpole's home was a 'theme park', and as such we can see it as the direct ancestor of Eerie Pubs.[6] Walpole's house formed part of a complex emerging ideology of consumption. He can be regarded as one of the earliest practitioners of a passion for interior design that has become one of contemporary British culture's biggest market forces, served by programmes like the BBC's *Changing Rooms*. Indeed, in his spin-off series, *Taste* (2002), the flamboyant *Changing Rooms* designer Laurence Llewellyn-Bowen paid tribute to Walpole in a special programme on Gothic, which also showed how to incorporate Gothic design into your bathroom. Gothic has become one out of many lifestyle choices: Eerie Pub or Irish Pub? Gothic light fittings or Urban Minimalism?

Eerie Pubs, therefore, need not be seen in the same light as their Irish equivalents. They are not 'selling out' an (arguably) once true and authentic experience, but are absolutely in keeping with Gothic as fake, as revival, as decor. Nevertheless, there is a sense in which these pubs also function like Disneyland, as described by Jean Baudrillard. For Baudrillard,

> Disneyland exists in order to hide that it is the 'real' country, all of 'real' America that *is* Disneyland . . . Disneyland is presented as imaginary in order to make us believe that the rest is real, whereas all of Los Angeles and the America that surrounds it are no longer real, but belong to the hyperreal order and the order of simulation.[7]

Eerie Pubs function to create the illusion that the 'original' Gothic is authentic; they produce nostalgia for the camp horror films from which they derive their aesthetics, or perhaps even the literary texts on which the films in turn were based. As Smith suggests above, this 'heritage Gothic' seems an empty version of the Gothic heritage it imitates. For Baudrillard, however, America is 'no longer' real. Gothic was never real in the first place. Gothic offers no resistance, as Romantic or Modernist ideologies might do, to being swallowed up by simulation, since its counterfeit nature pre-empts this move, even welcomes it. The very notion of 'mock Gothic' is a kind of oxymoron, because one cannot mock what is always already mocking itself.

The notion of mockery in the sense of parody is also vital here. Gothic and parody have always been close companions. The first phase of Gothic writing quickly elicited overt parodies, including Jane Austen's *Northanger Abbey* and Thomas Love Peacock's *Nightmare Abbey* (both 1818), but early texts like *The Castle of Otranto* and *The Monk* already appear to have a strong sense of their own ludicrousness, and deliberately incorporate comic episodes in imitation of Shakespearean tragedy. More recently, film and TV productions from *The Munsters* and *The Addams Family* to *Scary Movie* (a parody of the already parodic *Scream* movies), and more or less the entire œuvre of the film director Tim Burton, have continued in this tradition. *Sleepy Hollow* (1999), for instance, acknowledges the (often unintentionally funny) 1960s horror films of Roger Corman and the Hammer Studios in its deliberately hammy acting, over-exaggerated sets and slightly crumby special effects (the headless horseman becomes, in the later sequences of the film, increasingly ridiculous-looking). This does not work against the film but is part of its appeal – indeed, part of its Gothicity. Its knowingness, its signalling of its place within a particular tradition, permits it to combine humour with horror: the sequence in which the headless horseman pursues the hero Ichabod Crane combines farcical moments (such as Ichabod being knocked off the carriage with a tree branch) with genuine tension. The film never becomes an outright spoof, because its allegiance to the mode it gently parodies is too strong; it works instead to realize the comedy already latent within it. In *Gothic and the Comic Turn*, Avril Horner and Sue Zlosnik stress the hybridity of such texts, as well as Gothic's intrinsically comic nature: 'Rather than setting up a binary between "serious" and "comic" Gothic texts, it is perhaps best to think of Gothic writing as a spectrum that, at one end, produces horror-writing containing moments of comic hysteria or relief and, at the other, works in which there are clear signals that nothing is to be taken seriously.'[8] The shifts of tone inherent to the form are enabled, they argue, precisely by its lack of 'authenticity' or depth: 'Indeed, it is the Gothic's preoccupation with "surface" that enables it so easily to embrace a comic as well as a tragic perspective.'[9] For Horner and Zlosnik, the comic strain is becoming increasingly evident in Gothic novels written within the era of postmodernity. Certainly authors of the 'literary' Gothic, many of whom they discuss, seldom tell 'straight' horror stories any longer: Angela Carter, Patrick McGrath, Iain Banks and Alasdair Gray all write in the 'comic Gothic' mode, while 'serious' horror is left to 'popular' authors like Stephen King. The revival of Gothic in children's fiction, too, from Roald Dahl's *The Witches* (1983) to Lemony Snicket's *A Series of Unfortunate Events* (1999–), tends to make extensive use of the comic register.

The hollow laughter playing on an endless loop in the toilets of Eerie Pubs, therefore, is strangely resonant. It is laughter without a joke – the laughter itself is the joke. It does, in itself, provoke laughter – a hysterical response to one's own reaction of surprise, or because of its incongruity with the room's function (a new take on toilet humour). It is not laughing *at* what it copies, however, but with it – it is a joke that we all are in on.

Fake Histories, Fake Texts

Laughter of a more queasy kind is provoked by Jake and Dinos Chapman's *The Chapman Family Collection* (2002), an installation composed of a large group of apparently authentic 'primitive' masks and fetish objects, which resemble those found in an ethnographic museum. At first glance their verisimilitude is their most striking quality: composed of traditional materials, bristling with raffia and nails, they form a sinister group, evoking Western fears of 'primitive' religion, voodoo, idol worship and the colonial 'heart of darkness'. On closer inspection, however, details come into focus: one has the head of Ronald McDonald, another is shaped like a hamburger, others bear sinister markings that gradually resolve themselves into a repeated double-arched 'M'. *The Chapman Family Collection* is exemplary postmodern Gothic. Its tone is hard to ascertain, and the questions it asks are more frightening than any answers it can provide. Does the branding of these 'ancient' sculptures with the cheapest and most ubiquitous logo in Western culture diminish their power to frighten, by comically deflating their sinister aura, or does it increase it? Is the notion that our unconscious is globally branded a more chilling thought than that of a barbaric heart of darkness within the Western psyche? Is our authentic experience of trepidation or awe in front of these objects fatally adulterated by the brand? Is the inexorable apparatus of capitalism the chilling element here? The walking hamburgers and clown faces that McDonald's uses to sell its products to kids are themselves revealed as faintly chilling, Gothicized. The notion of history – that these objects have been collected by the Chapman family over many decades, perhaps centuries – is deflated by blatant anachronism. The apparent weight of history here is an illusion, a carefully orchestrated – and deliberately revealed – fake.

The construction of fake histories is integral to Gothic texts. As already noted, Walpole's *The Castle of Otranto* proclaimed itself as an 'authentic' manuscript from the twelfth century. Soon, the 'found manuscript' became a standard Gothic convention: the discovery of a lost or hidden document that reveals dreadful secrets concerning the fate of its author, before crumbling away just before the crucial point is made. This manuscript is often in poor condition, fragmented, missing important information. The narrator may be unreliable or inarticulate. It is often framed by supporting narratives that elaborate on or question the story told inside. Examples are to be found in Radcliffe's *The Romance of the Forest* (1791), Charles Maturin's *Melmoth, the Wanderer* (1820) and James Hogg's *The Private Memoirs and Confessions of a Justified Sinner* (1824) among others – and Jane Austen parodies the convention in *Northanger Abbey* by having her heroine, Catherine Morland, alight breathlessly on a hidden parchment, only to discover it is a laundry list. Contemporary authors have seized on this convention, from Emma Tennant's feminist rewrite of Hogg, *The Bad Sister* (1978), to Umberto Eco's presentation of *The Name of the Rose* (1980) as a translation of a rare fourteenth-century manuscript, a manoeuvre consonant with the novel's theme of the textual transmission of knowledge and its fallibilities. Alasdair Gray's *Poor Things* (1992), a fabulous comic Gothic rewriting of Hogg, Mary Shelley and Robert Louis Stevenson, among others, uses the convention to satirize the cultural and economic deprivation of Scotland in the 1970s: lacking money to purchase objects for the local history museum, assistant curator Michael Donnelly salvages materials from buildings scheduled for demolition to make way for multi-storey flats, and thus discovers the single surviving copy of the memoirs of Archibald McCandless, MD. Gray's novel is patch-worked together from letters and documents supposedly written in the nineteenth century and of which no originals exist: like Stoker's account of Dracula, merely 'a mass of typewriting'.

The 'found manuscript' theme has inevitably been transformed by the growth of information technologies: the labyrinthine intricacies of the World Wide Web creates the potential for all kinds of felicitous discoveries, while sophisticated word-processing programmes permit ever-more elaborate arrangements of texts. The employment of high modern technology in order to construct fake histories unites two of the most innovative and influential Gothic texts of recent years: Mark Z. Danielewski's *House of Leaves* (2000) and Daniel Myrick's and Eduardo Sanchez's film *The Blair Witch Project* (1998).

The Blair Witch Project infamously used the Internet in order to create a framing narrative for its tale of terror. In 1998 a rumour began to spread around the online community: three students had disappeared in a wood near Burkittsville, Maryland, while shooting a film about a sinister local legend for a college project. They were never found, but a year later their film footage was recovered. Images from this footage and evidence surrounding the case could be viewed on a dedicated website, flagging the eventual release of the re-edited footage in the form of a documentary. A sophisticated and, at the time, innovative form of promotion, the use of the Internet facilitated the growth of a kind of contemporary urban myth that blurred imperceptibly into hype when the entirely fictional film finally reached cinemas. The success of this Gothically inflected marketing strategy – the cultivation of fearful expectation through a kind of viral transmission – led to the film far exceeding its ultra-low-budget expectations, going on to take $150 million at the American box office alone, and becoming one of the most profitable films of all time. By the time it reached Europe the hype machine had taken over and bred a good deal of inevitable disappointment among audiences expecting to see 'the scariest movie ever made'. When the film was first screened in America, however, many viewers were apparently still unaware of its fictional status. *The Blair Witch Project* caused such an extreme reaction among its initial audiences because, like the radio broadcast *The War of the Worlds* sixty years earlier, it appeared to be true.

The Blair Witch Project uses many standard Gothic tricks. It provokes the imagination, suggesting the unspeakable rather than delivering it in full Technicolor. It uses the techniques of what the eighteenth-century Gothic novelist Ann Radcliffe might have approvingly called terror rather than horror, its frights implicit rather than explicit.[10] There are no special effects, no gore, in fact no appearance of the witch at all, simply tricks of shadow and sound, sinister impressions born out of the joint sensory disorientation of actors and audience. It is possible that those viewers who were reportedly underwhelmed by the experience were simply lacking in the imagination required to elaborate on the hints and clues the narrative offered (or simply weren't paying attention to details).

Most significantly, however, *The Blair Witch Project* concerns a found manuscript. *The Blair Witch Project* transfers this convention to cinema: the manuscript in this case is a set of videotapes and film reels – confused, unclear, inconclusive. What is more, these documents are supported by framing material in a range of media, including a further 'documentary', *Curse of the Blair Witch* (1999), and, of course, the accompanying website, which purported to display objectively the 'evidence' amassed by investigators, as well as explain the (invented) history of the Blair Witch – the only place where she does appear, being absent from the film itself. *The Blair Witch Project* is the quintessence of contemporary Gothic, a found manuscript for the information age. It deliberately exploits the audience's desire for the real, while simultaneously providing very little solid information: paradoxically, in this case, the very insubstantiality of the evidence available makes the story 'convincing'. The sequel, *Book of Shadows: Blair Witch II* (2000), provides a good deal more information about what happens to its particular teenage victims, and fails to replicate the illusion of authenticity. To follow Baudrillard's logic of simulacra, those fans turning up in the real-life town of Burkittsville hoping for a sight of the Blair Witch (which, interestingly, the sequel takes as the basis for its narrative) are not deceived, since in a media-saturated age the invented mythology of the Blair Witch has effectively become real: the legend has taken on a life of its own and requires no factual basis to support it.

'This Is Not For You'

Contemporary technology was also instrumental in the production of Mark Z. Danielewski's *House of Leaves*: the book was first serialized on the Internet, and the convoluted textual arrangements of the novel would have been near impossible to construct without a high-powered computer (Danielewski used a 300 Mhz G3 processor).[11] *House of Leaves* is the quintessential example of contemporary fiction in the Gothic mode, a novel that takes all the conventions and clichés of Gothic narratives and reorders them in spectacular fashion. Seven hundred pages long, riddled with thousands of footnotes, it is a bewildering collection of documents, a textual labyrinth. Like the house it describes, its dimensions constantly seem to shift and change as the narrative shifts from one textual level to another. At its centre is a film called *The Navidson Record*, a documentary shot by a photojournalist, Will Navidson, which traces his family's strange experiences in their new home in rural Virginia – not so far, geographically, from Burkittsville, Maryland. Returning from a trip away, the Navidsons discover a mysterious extra room in their house; upon measuring the house it seems that it is, impossibly, a quarter-inch bigger on the inside than it is on the outside. The dimensions of the house continue to shift, eventually opening up an apparently infinite labyrinthine space within its walls. In a textbook illustration of the Freudian uncanny, the 'homely' is shown to be unhomely, that which should be familiar made unfamiliar.

This film is the subject of the 'core' narrative, a critical commentary by an old man named Zampanò, discovered after his death by the 'editor' Johnny Truant, a trainee tattooist. Both these narrators are eminently unreliable: Zampanò because he is blind (and therefore cannot have seen the film he describes); Truant because he is apparently a pathological liar (his name ironically comprises phonetic connotations of 'true' or 'truth' and its literal meaning of 'shirking' or 'idle', a person missing from school or work). Truant's narrative of his discovery of the manuscript in Zampanò's apartment, the editing process and his ensuing madness, frames Zampanò's narrative and periodically interrupts it, in the form of scholarly footnotes, and footnotes to footnotes, which spiral off into stories about his own life. Some of these stories are self-consciously fictitious; others seem to be 'true' within the world of the text. Finally, anonymous 'editors' annotate both Zampanò's and Truant's narratives, and add appendices, including a further narrative told in epistolary form, that of Johnny Truant's mother. The relative fictionality or truth of what we are reading is constantly placed under interrogation, with different authorities contradicting and undermining one another. None of these narrators can be identified with Mark Z. Danielewski, whose name does not even appear on the title page, as if to preserve the integrity of his fictional narrators. Further, the titling of the book as *Mark Z. Danielewski's House of Leaves*, rather than *House of Leaves* by Mark Z. Danielewski, creates a shift in the conventional relationship between the author and their work. Danielewski does not seem to be the author of the book; rather he has produced or orchestrated it, in a manner more reminiscent of a film director. His responsibilities are diminished: he claims ownership of the work, but not necessarily authorship.

The form of the book itself also contributes to its labyrinthine nature. Some of the footnotes could be read as paradoxically conveying the main story, if Truant is considered as the central character. The text begins to disintegrate as the book progresses, some pages telling two or even three stories at the same time in different columns and boxes, some pages carrying only a single word or phrase. Some parts of the text are written backwards, so they can be read only in a mirror; others are crossed out. A letter is written in French, another in code that must be painstakingly deciphered by the reader. Tangled footnotes cause the reader to flip backwards and forwards between pages, mirroring the spatial confusion of the house itself, while in the most suspenseful parts of the story only a single word or phrase appears on each page, causing the reader physically to speed through these sections. In one part of the story, Will Navidson, lost in the lightless passages beneath his home, reads a book. That book is *House of Leaves*. Because his matches will not last long enough to enable him to read the whole book, he begins burning the pages he has already read to produce more light. When he reaches the final page, there are no other pages left, so he sets fire to the top of the page and reads it as it burns. Reading is figured as consumption; the page is literally consumed as Navidson metaphorically consumes it. Moreover, since the word 'leaf' can also mean 'page', by burning *House of Leaves* Navidson is also in effect burning down his own house. The book / house is a self-consuming artefact.

As if to convolute the textual labyrinth still further, Danielewski's sister, a musician named (with obvious Gothic resonance) Poe, concurrently released an album entitled *Haunted*, which provided an intertextual counterpoint to her brother's novel. The songs on *Haunted* were inspired by reading drafts of *House of Leaves*, although they often seem rather obliquely connected to the story, and the sleeve notes contain page references linking them (sometimes bafflingly) to the text. In addition, the album contains samples of a tape recording of the siblings' father that Poe found after his death. Although Poe's album mines a seam somewhere between that of the female singer-songwriter and polished adult pop, nothing like the 'Goth' music of the 1980s and '90s underground, nevertheless it is able to make a claim for being 'contemporary Gothic' in its concept and method of production. Poe's album is 'haunted' not only by her own family secrets hinted at through her father's ghostly utterances, but also by traces of its companion text, without which it is incomplete. The power of the text to cross the invisible boundary between page and reader is a constant theme of *House of Leaves*, from the obsession that Truant develops with Zampanò's story to the textual tricks that emphasize the physical experience of reading. At one crucial point in the book, the possibility of the minotaur – or whatever terrible monster Truant or the text is trying to repress – escaping the textual labyrinth and emerging in the reader's own reality becomes breathtakingly close, as Truant instructs the reader of a fearful presence on the periphery of their vision. Similarly, it becomes difficult, after reading *House of Leaves*, to listen to Poe's album without straining for ineffable words or sounds that might signal the presence of the novel. Furthermore, *House of Leaves* is reciprocally haunted: Poe's music makes a ghostly appearance towards the end of the book. Johnny Truant enters a bar where the band are playing a song with the lyric 'I live at the end of a five and a half minute hallway', a line from *Haunted*, that itself refers to the title of a short film discussed by Zampanò.[12] The hooking of choruses to textual references ensures that, when reading the book after listening to the album, Poe's tantalizing melodies echo through the reader's experience of the text.

The notion of reciprocal haunting does not end there: when Johnny meets the band after the show and asks them about the song, they tell him it was inspired by a book, and to his surprise hand him a copy of *House of Leaves*, with the warning "'It'll change your life.'"[13] Johnny recounts:

> Already, they had spent many hours with complete strangers shooting the shit about Zampanò's work. They had discussed

the footnotes, the names and even the encoded appearance of Thamyris on page 387, something I'd transcribed without ever detecting . . . During their second set, I thumbed through the pages, virtually every one marked, stained and red-lined with inquiring and I thought frequently inspired comments. In a few of the margins, there were even some pretty stunning personal riffs about the lives of the musicians themselves.[14]

In this scene, Johnny meets the readers of *House of Leaves*: readers who are not passive but whose questions and stories fill the margins of the pages. In the process of interpreting Zampanò's manuscript they become doubles of Johnny Truant, Charles Baudelaire' s 'Hypocrite lecteur, – mon semblable, – mon frère!'.[15] If the process of reading, and responding, to the text has changed their lives, so does their version of the manuscript change Johnny's: he reports, after reading it, that 'finally I fell into a sleep no longer disturbed by the past'.[16] This is exegesis as exorcism: only the process of annotation, and of being annotated in turn, appears to bring Johnny peace (at least temporarily) from the multiple spectres that haunt him.

Speculation about the mysterious presence at the centre of the labyrinth, as well as the origins of Johnny's hauntings, is encouraged by the text: early editions had the word 'minotaur' in red, as if offering a rag to a bull. Zampanò's account always offers the word in strike-through, possibly suggesting a further repression of what lies at the heart of the house, or possibly that the 'solution' to the mystery can only ever be under erasure, can never be accessed. Playing into a strand of contemporary Gothic that reads the return of the repressed in terms of childhood abuse, Johnny Truant hints at awful events in his past, the key to which appears to be his insane mother, incarcerated in a lunatic asylum when he was aged seven. The horror in Navidson's psyche, on the other hand, is linked to Delial (the phonetic similarity to 'denial' is surely not coincidental), a starving African child attended by vultures, of whom Navidson took a Pulitzer Prize-winning photograph. There is also a sense, however, in which Danielewski deliberately allows the source of horror to remain nameless, shapeless, so that it can be shaped to the individual fears brought to the text by the reader. In his Introduction, Johnny Truant predicts the effect that the text will have on the reader:

> You'll stand aside as a great complexity intrudes, tearing apart, piece by piece, all of your carefully conceived denials, whether deliberate or unconscious. And then for better or for worse you'll turn, unable to resist, though try to resist you still will, fighting with everything you've got not to face the thing you most dread, what is now, what will be, what has always come before, the creature you truly are, the creature we all are, buried in the nameless black of a name.[17]

As J. G. Ballard has remarked in a discussion of the films of David Cronenberg, 'the disturbing event we witnessed in the past is the experience of being alive'.[18] At the same time, the reader is suggestively expelled from the text, forbidden to enter: the dedication (written in Johnny Truant's 'Courier' typeface) simply states: 'This is not for you.' This anti-dedication automatically places the reader in exile, invoking both the uncanniness of otherness and the thrill of the forbidden book. We break a taboo simply by turning the page.

The book has a tendency to make those who encounter it active readers but passive critics. Readers may have to turn the book upside down to read parts of the story or project their own fears into the labyrinth, but it is difficult to analyse the book without merely repeating what is already within it. The length and density of Danielewski's novel produce a sensation in the reader analogous to that of the sublime: like the awe and sensory confusion produced in the Romantics by the sight of the Alps (or in Navidson and his companions by the scale and ineffability of the labyrinth), the book's dizzying contortions defy verbal or textual communication. The parodies of critical discourse (one particularly funny section has Karen Navidson interviewing Jacques Derrida, Harold Bloom, Camille Paglia, Anne Rice and Hunter S. Thompson for their critical response to the film) pre-empt critical response, presenting comically reductive versions of each critic's or author's point of view and thus mocking a sound-bite culture that would reduce the text to vulgar versions of one theory or another. Only the horror writer Stephen King 'gets' the short film that Karen shows him, surmising that the house is a real place and not merely an artistic construction. While this manoeuvre adds further levels to the fictionality of the text (a fictionalized version of the real King grasps the 'reality' of Danielewski's fictional film), it also perhaps indicates a degree of respect and acknowledgement of genre-belonging further indicated elsewhere. It is impossible not to place *House of Leaves* in the tradition of Charles Maturin, James Hogg, Nathanial Hawthorne and Edgar Allan Poe: all the generic features are present and correct, from the revenant histories of the characters' childhood traumas to the dizzying enclosure of the house itself, and the increasing disintegration of both the text itself and the individual subjects within it. This is a debt the text acknowledges even as it denies (in a footnote, of course). However, the book is also in the tradition of metatextual fictions, particularly those of Jorge Luis Borges, but also of Cervantes' *Don Quixote* and Laurence Sterne's *Tristram Shandy*. In its self-reflexivity, *House of Leaves* is an exemplary postmodern text. It is also an exemplary Gothic one. In this text the two coincide with consummate precision.

Spaces of Absence

The space described by the Navidson house of *House of Leaves* is an uncanny space, a paradoxical space, but also a space of absence. Lost in the featureless passages that proliferate within the house, Navidson is filled with joy at the apparent sighting of a window. Windows often form symbolic thresholds in Gothic texts, like the broken windowpane against which Lockwood drags the wrist of Cathy's ghost in Emily Brontë's *Wuthering Heights* (1847): in this case, the threshold is between the living and the dead. The window in the midst of the Navidson house, however, cannot mediate between two states because it is situated in the midst of nothingness to begin with:

> Climbing out onto a narrow terrace on the other side, Navidson, for the second time during Exploration #5, confronts that grotesque vision of absence . . . But as he turns to go back, he finds the window has vanished along with the room. All that remains is the ashblack slab upon which he is standing, now apparently supported by nothing: darkness below, above, and of course darkness beyond.[19]

Contemporary Gothic is fascinated by spaces of absence: spaces where, even within apparently easy reach of civilization, one could disappear without trace. The Navidson house is in rural Virginia; Burkittsville is in Maryland; these are comparatively populated parts of the United States in which it would be difficult to walk for two days, as the protagonists of *The Blair Witch Project* do, and not come across any sign of civilization. This is precisely the point; the woods should be a safe space, yet have become inexplicably unsafe, unfamiliar, uncanny. Early American Gothic was fascinated with the frontier, a liminal space between wilderness and civilization; as Allan Lloyd-Smith suggests, 'there is . . . a terror of the land itself, its emptiness, its implacability; simply a sense of its vast, lonely, and possibly hostile space that . . . ultimately, resists any rational explanation'.[20] The closing of the geographical frontier at the end of the twentieth century led to what Brian McHale calls the 'strategy of reimagining

America as an *interior* frontier', of which he considers L. Frank Baum's *The Wizard of Oz* (1900) the primary example, for its location of the magical kingdom of Oz impossibly *within* the state of Kansas.[21] The Navidson house, the Burkittsville woods, the Black Lodge of David Lynch's TV series *Twin Peaks* (1990–91), repeat this manoeuvre. Spaces without identity, spaces that are not places, these spaces respond to what in the over-populated Western world is one of the most disturbing (if all too common) occurrences: disappearance. The disappeared confound the logic of narrative, as they defeat closure. As Elizabeth Gaskell wrote in 1851, 'let me say I am thankful I live in the days of the Detective police; if I am murdered, or commit bigamy, at any rate my friends will have the comfort of knowing all about it'.[22] Those who disappear allow no such comfort.

The contemporary art world is also fascinated with interior frontiers and spaces of absence. Gregory Crewdson's photographic series *Twilight* (1998–2002) refers to a time of day that is liminal, between worlds. In his vision of small-town America, strange things happen in this half-lit world: a pregnant woman walks on her front lawn in her underwear; an Ophelia-like corpse floats in a flooded living room; a man hovers above the shafts of light coming from the peep-holes he has constructed in his floorboards; an adolescent girl stands at her window covered in moths. There are repeated motifs in the series: pregnancy, school buses, butterflies and moths, monstrous piles of flowers, holes in the floor. Most seem to evoke impermanency or transitional states. The essay by Rick Moody accompanying Crewdson's collected images makes much of the story that, as a child, Crewdson overheard his father giving psychoanalytic sessions through the floorboards in the family living room. Moody uses this incident to suggest Crewdson's interest in the Freudian uncanny, in '*something which ought to have remained hidden but has come to light*'.[23] The weirdest of Crewdson's images are often precisely those where nothing much seems to be happening, but yet something is slightly 'off' – a woman contemplating her reflection in her triple-panelled mirror, for example, is standing exactly in

Gregory Crewdson, *Untitled*, 2001, digital C-Print.

the centre of a dark patch that could be dried blood, or scorching, or mould. We are given the impression of having seen something we should not, of having spied on a private moment of horror.

With *Black Star* (2001–2), the Scottish artist Douglas Gordon, on the other hand, sets out to recreate this unsafe space in the experience of the viewer. Entering into a dark room, lit only by strips of ultraviolet light, the viewer hears a Scottish voice reading aloud from Hogg's tale of Doppelgängers and demonic possession, *The Private Memoirs and Confessions of a Justified Sinner* (1824). The only way to orient oneself within this perplexing space is to stand exactly in its centre, whereupon it is revealed that it takes the form of a five-pointed star – and the viewer standing in the position from which the Devil is traditionally summoned. It is hard to convey in writing the sinister experience of entering *Black Star*. One enters out of curiosity, in the same way as countless Gothic protagonists, only to find oneself manipulated by the construction of the space into a position of profound spiritual discomfort, in which superstition momentarily overtakes rationalism and teases faith. The space allows the experience of the uncanny to be played out: one is only permitted to comprehend one's surroundings, to feel the comfort of recognition, once one has reached a position guaranteed to provoke a sense of otherness and personal risk. To enter the space is to enter into a pact with the artist in which he, like the Devil, is likely to have the upper hand.

Vampire Topographies

Concerns with empty spaces and the culture of simulation are united in Michael Almereyda's film of 1994, *Nadja*, a highly ironic and self-aware reworking of the vampire tradition. The vampire has become one of the predominant motifs of contemporary Gothic: although it came relatively late to the Gothic novel, making little impact before Polidori's reworking of the Byron myth in *The Vampyre* (1819), the narratives of J. Sheridan le Fanu's 'Carmilla' (1872) and Bram Stoker's *Dracula* (1897) are now endlessly reinterpreted and recycled in both cheap paperbacks and big-budget movie productions. Anne Rice's *Vampire Chronicles* (1976–2003), in particular, were responsible for fuelling the popular preoccupation with vampires, her series of 'memoirs' providing her vampires with an interior life and constructing them to resemble celebrities in whose lifestyles her readership can sustain a vicarious interest. Writing in 1994, Ken Gelder estimated that approximately 3,000 vampire films had been made so far, and there is no sign that they are diminishing in popularity.[24] With this level of exposure, it would seem that there is a danger of the vampire narrative falling prey to its own central metaphor and being sucked dry of invigorating life, doomed to replicate itself as empty cliché.

Almereyda's film offers a response to this impasse by implicitly making connections between vampires and Baudrillardian simulacra. In the film, Dracula himself is no longer representable: he appears merely as a silhouette on a cliff-top or, still more effectively, as inter-cut footage of Bela Lugosi (interestingly, not from his famous performance as Dracula). Dracula has been replaced by his own image, and Bela Lugosi has become the authentic Dracula, his instant recognition factor more powerful than Stoker's narrative, the copy replacing the original. Van Helsing compares Dracula to Elvis, that other undead figure of the American imagination, and another figure whose myth seems to have replaced his real-life existence. Elsewhere in the film Lucy stays up all night, not drinking blood but making endless photocopies, an oblique reference to the process of vampire reproduction, a form of copying or cloning rather than producing an original. It is suggested that vampire mythology has become so familiar to the viewer that it can be presented to us only ironically, in quotation marks – or made strange through the blurry images created by PixelVision, Almereyda's signature technique, which inter-cuts footage shot with a Fisher Price child's toy camera. The film is also profoundly concerned with space, echoing Fredric Jameson's argument that under the conditions of late capitalism daily life is governed by concepts of space rather than time.[25] Nadja, being undead, is no longer concerned with time and is therefore the ideal postmodern subject.

The opening sequence of the film comprises a haunting, multiple superimposition of Nadja's face, skyscrapers, smoke and fast-moving lights. To the sound of the psychedelic guitar band My Bloody Valentine, Nadja intones in voiceover, 'Nights – nights without sleep – long nights in which the brain lights up like a big city.' The film continues with a scene in which Nadja picks up a man in a bar: an apparently banal conversation between the two young people is ironicized as the viewer gradually realizes that the

Karl Geary as Renfield and Elina Löwensohn as Nadja in a still from Michael Almereyda's *Nadja* (1994).

woman is a vampire, the clichés of vampirism transposed into a contemporary setting. Accents and the names of major cities signify a global community, but otherwise the location remains markedly non-specific. Nadja dismisses Europe as 'a village' and goes on to praise what seems to be (but is not explicitly confirmed as) New York: 'Here, you feel so many things rushing together – it gets even more exciting after midnight.' Her partner asks her if she finds it hectic, and she responds: 'Sometimes I need to get away – I want to be alone without this confusion – a tree, a lake, a dog'.

The first few moments of the film thus present an intense consciousness that has, in a sense, replaced the external landscape. Nadja's face is superimposed with the lights of the metropolis even as she claims these lights as a metaphor for her own nocturnal experiences. For the vampire the brain itself becomes the landscape; external world and internal experience are merged to such an extent that they become inextricable, two topographies occupying identical space. This is reminiscent of Edgar Allan Poe's fiction, in which it is often difficult to tell where the narrator's internal world stops and the external world begins: landscape exists to reflect back the obsessions and preoccupations of the speaker and contains no external reference points, the placeless House of Usher being the most obvious example. Within this personalized space local particulars are lost, and are reduced to archetypes: 'a big city', 'a tree'. This intangibility of landscape is sustained throughout the film, the blurred focus of PixelVision working to prevent the establishing of coherent cinematic space in a similar manner to the hand-held cameras of *The Blair Witch Project*.

Nadja makes numerous references to other vampire films, but one of the most important is F. W. Murnau's *Nosferatu* of 1922, which is evoked through a series of staircase shots in which the vampire's distorted shadow moves slowly across a wall. Significantly, *Nosferatu* is celebrated for its innovative use of outdoor location filming, which was actually a result of the low budget prohibiting the construction of complicated sets. Paradoxically, however, this tends towards the emptying of landscape in much the same way as *Nadja*'s similarly low-budget indeterminacy of location. The film critic Eric Rhode notes of *Nosferatu* that when the vampire, played by Max Schreck, 'emerges high on the edge of the horizon, or framed in a doorway, or walking the deck of a ship, he seems to take possession of these places and rob them of their identity. Coffins and doorways become apt niches for his emaciated body, and bare fields seem to extend from his emaciated form.'[26] The vampire empties out landscape by his presence, in fact aptly 'vampirizes' it, draining it of independent existence.

Thus in *Nadja* the Black Sea is evoked by some nondescript water, the Carpathian Mountains by the silhouette of a nondescript cliff-top. Similarly, Nadja's description of a desired escape from the urban environment is simply 'a tree, a lake, a dog'. Spaces become interchangeable, identified through generalized, universal objects. In an early exchange

Lucy asks Nadja if her brother lives in Carpathia: 'No, Brooklyn', she replies. 'I've never been there. Have you?' Lucy says: 'Brooklyn? Once. No, actually twice, a long time ago.' From her blank expression, Brooklyn could be as distant as Carpathia, and as exotic. As for Nadja's birthplace, it is invoked repeatedly with the formula 'By the Black Sea, under the shadow of the Carpathian mountains', reminiscent of both the formulaic nature of vampire narrative and the glib descriptions of a guidebook. The line is not supported by images that reinforce the statement; rather, by a grainy, indistinct picture of a storybook castle. The vampire lives in a kind of hyper-real environment in which the sign has become more present than the landscape it represents.

Similarly, the location of Lucy's and Jim's home in Greenwich Village is only indicated by a literal sign: the name of the 24-hour copy-shop, the *Village Copier*. Ironically, this one concession to the specificity of place is a shop dedicated to the continual production of simulacra. Furthermore, this label ironically undercuts Nadja's own description of Europe as a 'village', with America in contrast as an adrenalin-fuelled metropolis, again pointing to the interchangeability of spaces in the 'global village'. Location is simultaneously indicated and denied. Significantly, the nurse Cassandra's evocation of Ireland as the 'land of music' is challenged by Renfield's self-contradictory retort: 'No, snakes. There's no snakes there. Never have been.' (A remark that itself appears to contradict the legend of St Patrick banishing the snakes from Ireland.) Place undoes itself, becomes a space defined only through absence.

It emerges in the course of the narrative that Nadja has come to New York with the same hopes and expectations as a whole history of immigrants, and of immigrant vampires – recalling what is virtually a subgenre of primarily comic films such as *Blacula* (1972), *Love at First Bite* (1979) and *A Vampire in Brooklyn* (1995). At one point Lucy mentions that her father is 'born again', which Nadja appears to understand in a rather different light, but the phrase has resonance throughout the film, as a metaphor for beginning a new life – for Nadja, tantamount to discovering a New World. Released by her father's death, she states: 'I am free and I can live a new life. I can start over. I'll find someone. I'll be happy.' Romantic love, for both Nadja and her father, is constructed as a means of changing one's identity equivalent to the American mythology of self-creation. (This is a theme reprised in *Love at First Bite*, in which Dracula, kicked out of Transylvania by the Communists, comes to the United States to find true love.) Van Helsing talks of Dracula's one true love using the same rhetoric with which Nadja talks of the possibilities of New York: 'He thought things were possible – a new life.' Yet this dream is denied by the film – at least while Nadja remains in America. She returns to Romania disillusioned, stating to Renfield: 'America was getting somehow – too confusing. Didn't you feel that? Too many choices – too many possibilities.' In America, signs proliferate, like the photocopies Lucy mindlessly makes or the grotesque toy vampire hanging on her Christmas tree. Europe, on the other hand, represents simplicity, the 'tree, a lake, a dog' of Nadja's longing. However, this simplicity is also shown by the film to be an over-determined construct, and ultimately inaccessible.

Contemporary geography has made much of the assertion that, as Derek Gregory puts it, 'mapping is necessarily situated, embodied, partial: *like all other practices of representation*'.[27] In the Hammer film of 1965, *Dracula, Prince of Darkness*, the authority of the conventional map is shown to be fallible when it comes to vampiric spaces. A party of travellers on their way to Karlsbad are warned away from a nearby castle by a local priest. The head of the party responds: 'Castle – but there's no castle marked on the map, I would have noticed!' With an ominous look, the priest replies: 'Because it is not on the map does not mean it does not exist – stay away from it!' Hammer films tend to stress the link between vampirism and Victorian sexual repression; indeed, it could be argued that they are largely responsible for the now-conventional reading of vampire narratives according to this model. Here repression is figured in spatial terms, as territory uncovered by the map – a fantastic space outside the symbolic order, where Dracula's libidinous forces are at work.

Thirty years later, however, it is impossible to represent vampirism in quite such an innocent way, since Hammer films themselves have contributed to the uncovering of all the uncharted spaces on the map, so the audience is all too aware of what they contain. As Baudrillard states: 'When there is no more territory virgin and therefore available for the imaginary, when the map covers the whole territory, then something like a principle of reality disappears.'[28] Thus, in *Nadja*, the flight to Romania is represented by the conventional cinematic signifier of a map, but in this case the country clearly marked 'Transylvania' in Gothic script is superimposed by Lucy's sinister, wailing vampire toy, highlighting both its artificially constructed nature and its over-determined status as a sign. The map simultaneously covers everything and nothing, and has no power to indicate anything beyond itself. It has entered the realm of the hyper-real: as Baudrillard again argues, in the postmodern state 'the real is not only what can be reproduced, but *that which is always already reproduced*'.[29] A map is obviously always already a reproduction, but in this case the territory that it reproduces, 'Transylvania', is not a 'real' referent but a product precisely of the map itself. This is reinforced by the fact that the first shot of Nadja's home country shows a child playing in a forest wearing Mickey Mouse ears. We are no longer in Europe, but in Euro Disney.

Within this environment humans and vampires begin to seem equally undead: they are all locked in the same empty cycles of behaviour, endlessly repeating the same patterns. Nevertheless, the film does tentatively offer a way out. The end of *Nadja* sees the soul of the dead vampire mysteriously transfused into the body of Cassandra. Nadja is literally born again as an American. However, the theme of double-exposure, of two topographies occupying the same space, translates into a kind of double-consciousness, two voices within the same head. The image that began the film, of Nadja's face superimposed by the lights of the city, is replaced by Cassandra's face superimposed by sunlight, leaves and water – the tree and lake of Nadja's desire. Finally, Cassandra's face merges into Nadja's. 'Who's there – is it only me? Is it myself?' the voice of Nadja / Cassandra asks. The scene seems to find hope in the notion of hybrid identity, but also leaves a lingering sense of the uncanny: Nadja / Cassandra have become 'other' to themselves, alien territory.

In becoming 'born again' in the body of a living woman, the vampire as simulacra enacts a suggestive return to the real, an embodiment. While the questioning nature of the final voice-over suggests the tentative, provisional nature of this reinstatement of the human, other Gothic texts have directly confronted the status of the body in the era of simulation. For Jerrold Hogle, this is one of the most radical and politically significant features of contemporary Gothic:

> Terror can return . . . in a fantasy that deliberately strives to point out *the body*, indeed the most primal and destructible possibilities of the body, and thereby recover it from earlier Gothic disembodiments and the dissolution of it into myriad simulations, large and small. The 'otherness' of the body from the simulacra that would suck out its life, simulacra of the sort that some have used to deny the physical reality of the Holocaust, is reasserted by these 'new Gothic' writers and film-makers.[30]

Contemporary Gothic discourses are in this respect dual-natured: in their emphasis on surfaces, they may offer a lack of resistance to simulation; but in their foregrounding of the body they offer scope for their use in an entirely opposite way, for the reinstatement of depth into a superficial culture. While not all contemporary Gothic productions can be regarded in this way, there is a sizeable minority of texts and films that play out the tension between physical or spiritual embodiment and the dominance of the sign, and these form the subject of the next chapter.

CHAPTER TWO

Grotesque Bodies

Fake Plastic Corpses

In 2002 the biggest sensation to hit London was *Body Worlds*, Gunther von Hagens's travelling exhibition of dissected and elaborately displayed corpses. Preserved by his newly developed method of 'plastination', whereby all bodily fluids are pumped out of the body and replaced with plastic, the bodies were positioned in a variety of poses designed to show off the wonder of the human form, from a 'swimmer' and a 'chess player' to the pièce de résistance, a man astride a full-sized plastinated horse. Predictably, von Hagens's show divided audiences. While many saw it as a glorious celebration of the human body and a unique chance for improving the scientific knowledge of the masses, others objected to a variety of factors: from the allegedly dubious provenance of some of the bodies to the queasy commercialization of the exhibition, and the lack of female bodies on display (a fact initially explained by von Hagens himself as due to the relative lack of female donors, and later, somewhat defensively, as due to apprehensiveness concerning voyeurism). Von Hagens's all-consuming obsession with plastination could not avoid appearing sinister on a Channel 4 documentary profiling his career – his wife readily admitting,

Gunther von Hagens and a plastinated horse at the *Body Worlds* exhibition at the Atlantis Gallery, London, 2002.

without apparent irony, that he would choose plastination over her – and he soon became known in the media as a kind of latter-day Dr Frankenstein.[1] Frankenstein, of course, aimed to build new life out of his corpses, which von Hagens does not pretend to do, although he does portray the plastination process as a kind of life-in-death, a form of immortality of the body, if not the soul. Gothic echoes surrounded the London show, which was housed in a converted warehouse in Whitechapel, just round the corner from the sites of Jack the Ripper's infamous crimes of the 1880s, and close to the location of the sideshow that exhibited Joseph Merrick, the 'Elephant Man', in the same period. The controversy surrounding the show, which von Hagens claimed was entirely absent in most other countries in which he had exhibited, was caused in no small part by the cultural context in which it took place. Nevertheless, Hagens, a consummate showman, appeared to thrive on the frisson of historical transgression.

The bodies on display were rigorously stripped of any personal identifying features: identity was subordinated to science. In this way what was apparently intended as a celebration of humanity seemed to jettison that very humanity: it became difficult to distinguish the bodies from sophisticated plastic dummies. The spectacle of death became clinical, detached, emotionless. The frisson of the 'real' that von Hagens's publicity promised was oddly diminished, and further mitigated by the white space of the gallery and strategic potted plants. Despite the media frenzy, the exhibition contained few horror-show thrills: this was a Disneyfied death, purged of all its messiness.

It is difficult to discuss an exhibition like *Body Worlds* without incorporating personal response. The material deliberately positions the spectators to make comparisons with their own bodies, in the tradition of the *memento mori*: 'as I am now so you will be'. Individual reactions to the corpses were one of the most interesting things about the exhibition, as suggested by the crowds hunched around the comments book at the end.

For me, one figure in the exhibition provoked a slightly different response to that of detached curiosity. His cadaver was divided into perfect vertical slices, the identifying skin of his face removed, in common with all von Hagens's bodies. Yet his body remained marked, with a variety of now-blurry tattoos. He would have remained recognizable to anyone who had known him well. Skin is the repository of experience; the marks and lines that appear upon it tell a story about that body's identity. For me and my companions at least, this was the single exhibit to provoke an emotion other than curiosity and vague distaste, and to cross a line (among others) between science and art – for long before von Hagens's intervention, this man had attempted to make his own body into a work of art, however crude the results may have been. This was a body that had made choices and displayed the consequences of those choices; it was a body that sought to modify itself, to present itself in a particular way. In death, his body became discomforting, even shocking, for it still possessed traces of an identity other than that imposed by the master doctor.

Von Hagens's massively successful exhibition, attended by 840,611 visitors in London alone, illustrates a contradiction within contemporary Gothic. Its flayed and dissected bodies, animated with a ghastly semblance of life, recall literary revenants like Frankenstein's Creature and Dracula. However, divested of a history, plasticized, dangled in pristine white gallery space, the bodies lack any of the more traditional social or psychic resonances we expect from Gothic phenomena. They do not (for most viewers, at least) provoke the extreme emotions of horror or disgust more usually associated with Gothic bodies. They are stripped of affect in a similar way to that described by Fred Botting, who suggests that traditional objects of horror have become over-exposed to the point of banality: 'Unless the horror is spectacular no interest will be excited: human feeling is extinguished or anaesthetised or boredom sets in.'[2] On one level, perhaps, this is as it should be: von Hagens has no interest in presenting his work as Gothic, appealing instead to the 'objective' discourses of anatomical science; the association with the infamous body-snatchers Burke and Hare or Frankenstein is a media construction. The *Body Worlds* cadavers are grotesque rather than Gothic: a conglomeration of bodily process and the macabre jokiness of postmodern Carnival. Yet in the single instance when the traces of history, in the form of personal experience, are allowed to creep back into the frame, then a moment of uncanny recognition occurs (this was once a person like me – familiar – but now is unfamiliar – dead and dissected).

Contemporary Gothic is more obsessed with bodies than in any of its previous phases: bodies become spectacle, provoking disgust, modified, reconstructed and artificially augmented. On one level this treatment of the body seems coextensive with the Gothic simulations and artifice described in the last chapter. Gothic bodies are frequently presented to us as simulations, as replacements of the real. Von Hagens's plastic corpses retain almost none of the 'original' body tissue; flesh has literally been replaced by plastic. While not what Baudrillard would term pure simulacra, in that they do retain a relationship with the 'original', evidencing a desire to illustrate a body constructed as 'real', they simultaneously appear to evacuate all sense of nostalgia for personal history. Elevated into archetypes such as 'swimmer' or 'reclining woman', the beings inhabiting Von Hagens's brave new world are idealized, perfected, sterile, monstrous.

Elsewhere, contemporary artists more self-consciously present the human body in terms of simulacra. Jake and Dinos Chapman's *Great Deeds Against the Dead* reproduces Goya's sketch of mutilated war-time corpses as sculpture, with cartoonish plastic dummies standing in for his closely observed bodies. Through incessant media representation, the Chapmans' version has arguably become (at least temporarily) the better-known image, replacing not only the 'original' bodies, invested with historical and political significance, but also Goya's 'original' representation of them. The Chapmans' mutant child mannequins, which are fused into freakish hybrid beings, with anuses for mouths and penises for noses, have a similar effect.

Jake and Dinos Chapman, *Great Deeds Against The Dead*, 1994, mixed media.

Interestingly, they caused less controversy at the *Sensation* exhibition at the Royal Academy in 1997 than Marcus Harvey's giant, iconic portrait of the 'Moors Murderer' Myra Hindley, created from children's handprints. Harvey's image, a striking comment on media representation, lent itself both to re-representation within the media and to desecration in a way that the grotesque bodies of the Chapman Brothers' already-defiled children did not. Both artworks tapped into a current moral panic surrounding childhood innocence, but whereas Harvey provided a scapegoat, the Chapmans attacked the myth fuelling this panic, denying it currency. The mutant children running and playing in the plastic Eden of *Tragic Anatomies*, wearing identical white trainers, suggested the artificiality of our fantasies of Rousseau-esque innocence, proffering instead the lush beauty of a poisoned world. As in *Great Deeds Against the Dead*, the Chapmans' child bodies are simulacra: they belong to their own, autonomous, synthetic realm, their artificiality reproducing nothing more than the constructedness of our cultural concepts of childhood.

Alternatively, it could be argued that contemporary Gothic's preoccupation with freaks, scars, diseased flesh, monstrous births and, above all, blood is an attempt to reinstate the physicality of the body in an increasingly decorporealized information society. The Chapmans' *Great Deeds Against the Dead* could be matched by Mark Quinn's *Head*, also shown in *Sensation*. A self-portrait moulded from eight pints of the sculptor's frozen blood, the object seems to offer an intimacy, an uncanny physical presence, that troubles the division between the 'representation' and the 'real'.

In this respect Gunther von Hagens's *Body Worlds* show illustrates some of the contradictions that surround our thinking about bodies in contemporary Gothic. The corpses in the exhibition, in their stylized poses, are putting on a performance without their own agency, as if manipulated by the strings of a deranged puppet-master. Their grotesquerie treads a fine line between the natural – the gory inner workings of the body – and the artificial – the creative agency of the dissector's knife, and the inexorability of his plastic-pumping contraption. Human yet plastic, Von Hagens's bodies are both real and a replacement of the real. They are poised on the boundary between art and science, education and entertainment, celebration and exploitation, detachment and disgust. Above all, in the 40,000 people world-wide who have signed up to donate their own corpses, they demonstrate our willingness to make a spectacle of ourselves.

The traditional Christian belief in bodily resurrection has been replaced by the notion of a secularized resurrection as show, with physical immortality the pay-off rather than a spiritual one. Whereas once Gothic fiction was generated around the idea that one's body might be abducted and dissected against one's wish, as in Robert Louis Stevenson's famous tale 'The Body-Snatcher' (1884), now individuals are queuing up to be dissected in a bid for a kind of deathly celebrity.

Gothic and Grotesque

The public embrace of Von Hagens's dubious offer of immortality points to another significant theme in contemporary Gothic: the democratization of monstrosity. Plastination is no longer the dreadful thing that happens to someone else, like the artificially preserved victims of the early Vincent Price film *House of Wax* (1953), but a lifestyle (deathstyle?) choice one might actively select. Our attitude to monstrous bodies has shifted in the West. While the freakish may always have inspired a complex mixture of fear and desire, as Leslie Fiedler has argued, they no longer represent images of what he memorably terms our 'secret self', but explicitly shape our identities.[3] Moreover, the treatment of the monstrous and grotesque has notably become lighter and more irreverent in a significant number of texts: bodily difference is seen as a cause for joy and celebration in a new inflexion of what the Russian theorist Mikhail Bakhtin has termed 'Carnival'.

Bakhtin most famously outlines this theory in *Rabelais and His World* (1965). Carnival, the medieval 'feast of fools', is notable for its disruptive laughter, its reversal of conventional hierarchies and its emphasis on the material or grotesque body. The grotesque body is a body in process: a bizarre, exaggerated, hyperbolic body, fragmented and dismembered, distinguished by its protuberances and orifices. It is implicitly opposed to the 'classical' body, or that associated with the dominant worldview of the Middle Ages, which is whole, completed, smooth, closed-off from the world and from other bodies. Within the limited space of the Carnival festivities, the raucous bodily humour associated with the grotesque may temporarily disrupt or overturn conventional hierarchies of power, so that, for instance, the effigy of the pope may be shown with enlarged genitals or a bare behind. The carnivalesque body is therefore associated with the voice of the underclass, and as such is considered to have subversive potential by many critics. Mary Russo, for example, views Carnival as 'a site of insurgency'. She argues that

> The masks and voices of carnival resist, exaggerate, and destabilize the distinctions and boundaries that mark and maintain high culture and organised society . . . The political implications of this heterogeneity are obvious: it sets carnival apart from the merely oppositional and reactive. Carnival and the carnivalesque suggest a redeployment or counterproduction of culture, knowledge and pleasure.[4]

Carnival always exists in dialogue with official culture, and as such offers potential for change, even if we accept that, historically, sometimes Carnival can become institutionalized and function to confirm official culture through a contained period of steam-letting. The grotesque body, likewise, is characterized by its fluidity and openness to things outside itself; it is 'blended with the world, with animals, with objects'.[5]

Gothic and the grotesque, in its Bakhtinian sense, are by no means coincident. As Chris Baldick and Robert Mighall argue in their essay on 'Gothic Criticism', notions of Gothic literature 'as a kind of "revolt" against bourgeois rationality, modernity or Enlightenment' are largely a product of twentieth-century criticism and cannot be sustained by an appeal to historically grounded evidence.[6] While Gothic is certainly 'popular' in terms of its mass appeal and lack of cultural prestige, it is not the product of a disenfranchised underclass in the sense that Bakhtin refers to; histor-ically, it is chiefly a product of middle-class culture. Furthermore, grotesque bodies in Gothic are not always comic or affirmative of the life of the body and the people – in fact, they are more frequently sinister and disturbing. Bakhtin includes the eighteenth- and nineteenth-century Gothic novel in his genealogy of the grotesque under the label of the 'Romantic Grotesque', which he describes as a reaction against Enlightenment classicism. The Romantic Grotesque is distinguished by its relinquishment of the commu-nal, 'folk' nature of the medieval and Renaissance grotesque to become 'an individual carnival, marked by a vivid sense of isolation'.[7] The joyous, triumphant laughter of earlier forms of Carnival is 'cut down to cold humor, irony, sarcasm', losing its positive regenerating power.[8] The Romantic Grotesque is sombre and sterile, and conveys terror rather than laughter. For Bakhtin, this form of the grotesque persisted throughout the nineteenth century and can be seen particularly in the attitude towards death exhibited by Victorian culture.

In contemporary Gothic, however, something of the 'original' spirit of Carnival seems to have returned. Contemporary fictions demonstrate a preoccupation with the 'folk' grotesque of the circus, with freakish heroes and heroines and with celebration of bodily excess. Nevertheless, these fictions retain their more Romantic / Gothic associations as well, in the Frankensteinian theme of Katherine Dunn's *Geek Love* (1983), for instance, or the sinister occult figures that pursue Fevvers, the winged heroine of Angela Carter's *Nights at the Circus* (1984). The two are melded in what might be termed the 'Gothic-Carnivalesque'. Gothic, Avril Horner and Sue Zlosnik suggest, is a hybrid form and embraces laughter as well as horror. They argue that 'it is precisely because the Gothic is always liminal and poised on boundaries – and already halfway to sending itself up – that its characteristic features can easily be turned to comic effect. Thus its tendency to the sinister grotesque is easily converted to the comic flamboyance of the grotesque as excess.'[9] In what I am calling the 'Gothic-Carnivalesque', the sinister is continually shading into the comic and vice versa. The film director Tim Burton works repeatedly in this mode: his anarchic spirit Betelguese (from the film *Beetlejuice*, of 1988), for example, with his slapstick approach to haunting, is simultaneously funny and frightening. However, these texts exhibit a crucial difference from both the Carnival tradition as Bakhtin describes it, and from much of the Gothic tradition too. Combining a wholly modern notion of the individual subject with the openness to the other found within the carnivalesque, one of the most prominent features of the new 'Gothic-Carnivalesque' is sympathy for the monster.

Monsters R Us

The monstrous 'other' has been a recurrent feature of Gothic narratives at least since the early nineteenth century, with the monstrous Creature of Mary Shelley's *Frankenstein* (1818) the most significant prototype. Traditional Gothic machinery – sublime landscapes, frame narratives, horrific murders – abound in the text, but the twin notions of a scientist who overreaches himself to create artificial life and a monster able to tell the story of his sufferings are those that drive the narrative and, in turn, power contemporary Gothic. As Chris Baldick and Fred Botting have variously argued, in the nineteenth century the story of Frankenstein grew beyond its source novel to become a modern myth.[10] Via James Whale's evocative films, *Frankenstein* (1931) and *Bride of Frankenstein* (1935), with Boris Karloff playing the Creature, Frankenstein and his monster have become ubiquitous and instantly recognizable metaphors for a plethora of contemporary conditions. From plastination to plastic surgery, cyborgs to genetically modified foods, *Frankenstein* provides a ready-made narrative. While many of these interpretations may, in actual fact, bear little relation to the story as told by Shelley, the term 'Frankenstein' has become common currency for both overreaching science and an archetypal human monster.

Perhaps the most intriguing thing about Shelley's novel, however, in terms of its contemporary influence, is the sympathy the monster elicits. The Creature – he has no name – tells his creator a story of ostracism, prejudice and withheld human contact. Articulate and well read, he is a powerful advocate of the human right to love and be loved. Unlike other nineteenth-century Gothic monsters – Quasimodo, Carmilla, Mr Hyde – Frankenstein's Creature elicits not only fascination or even sympathy, but also empathy. Allowed a voice, he becomes possible to identify with; whereas with Carmilla, Dracula or Hyde, ultimately their otherness is reconfirmed; they are vanquished, and the dominant social order ratified. As Fred Botting suggests, it is the monster, and not his creator, with whom twentieth- and twenty-first-century subjects align themselves: in a world in which the workings of science and technology seem increasingly opaque to ordinary individuals, Frankenstein provides a convenient metaphor for articulating a relationship with science. From this perspective, 'no longer are humans positioned on the side of science as it appropriates the secrets of life in the mastery of nature. Instead, identifying with the monster, humans are aligned with all that can be made and remade by a more than human technology.'[11]

In the twentieth century, the Frankenstein story is increasingly told from the monster's point of view. No longer marginalized and contained by the voice of his creator, the Creature takes over the narrative. Tod Browning's *Freaks* (1932), for example, creates a community of monsters who ultimately are also creators of monsters. A beautiful, blond aerialist marries a midget for his money and then humiliates and attempts to poison him, only to receive a terrible revenge on behalf of the circus freaks, who transform her into the hideous 'bird woman'. The freaks, all played by their 'real-life' counterparts, are part of a community that, within the confines of the circus, is the norm. The trapeze artist fails to understand

Director Tod Browning on set with members of the cast of *Freaks* (1932).

this, perceiving her own stereotypal femininity and the corresponding stylized masculinity of her accomplice, the strong man, as normal and her tiny lover as deviant. She resists the freaks' welcoming chant, 'One of us!, One of us!', and is forcibly inducted into the freak community as punishment. Browning's film demonstrates an odd ambivalence of tone: while the freaks are treated sympathetically, and it is true that Cleopatra's cruelty makes her the bigger freak even before her mutilation, the final scene in which they slither, hobble and crawl through the mud of a thunderstorm towards their victim deliberately plays on the disturbing sense of otherness produced by their physical appearances.

In Katherine Dunn's novel *Geek Love*, the tale of a family of circus freaks named the Binewskis, constructed Frankenstein-like by their parents through a series of narcotic experiments during pregnancy, 'Arturo the Amazing Aquatic Boy' justifies to his sister Olympia (a bald, hunchbacked, albino dwarf) his love of ghost stories and horror tales:

And do you know what the monsters and demons and rancid spirits are? Us, that's what. You and me. We are the things that come to the norms in nightmares. The thing that lurks in the bell tower and bites out the throats of the choirboys – that's you, Oly. And the thing in the closet that makes the babies scream in the dark before it sucks their last breath – that's me . . . These books teach me a lot. They don't scare me because they're about me. Turn the page.[12]

Geek Love demonstrates a shift in sensibilities. The monster is no longer the other. Olympia's narrative is not protectively sandwiched between those of her creator and his confidant, like that of her fictional ancestor, Frankenstein's Creature, but is allowed to take over the whole book. While she certainly encounters prejudice from 'norms', her own narrative pleasingly overturns conventional hierarchies so that to be a 'norm' is, paradoxically, to be strange. In Olympia's family, only those babies without any apparent defects are to be discarded, in an inversion of the conventional cultural attitude to freaks. The more freakish the baby, the more prized it is, so that Olympia's own deformities, relatively banal besides those of her brothers and sisters, are a source of sorrow to her precisely because she is not quite freakish *enough*. Indeed, as the novel progresses, Arturo becomes the head of a cult known as 'Arturism', in which norms seek deliverance from their everyday problems by becoming more like him: by amputating their limbs. The norms long to be freaks; if they cannot be born freaks, like Olympia and Arturo, they will allow themselves to be made into them. Among Arturo's disciples are two bikers, who, once their arms have been removed, carefully dry and preserve their tattooed skin. In their quest to become freaks, amputation is a logical outcome to a trajectory of more conventional body modification practices.

Geek Love is in fact full of Frankenstein figures: different people seeking to create monsters for different motives. Besides the Binewski parents, and the megalomaniac Arturo with his sinister self-trained surgeon Dr P., there is also Mary Lick, a philanthropist heiress who aims to help women achieve their full potential by performing operations that rid them of all sexual attractiveness. Scarred and neutered, her protégées become scientists and astronauts, like the Arturan amputees their minds freed from their troublesome bodies. Both Arturism and Mary Lick satirize our culture's preoccupation with changing our lives through changing our bodies, seen in insidious form in the pages of numerous dieting manuals and magazines. Yet despite this apparent contempt for the flesh, it appears difficult to leave the body behind in *Geek Love*, just like the failed experiments that the Binewskis carry with them in glass jars wherever they go, or the brain-dead lump of a Siamese twin that Iphy, her sister, is compelled to carry around with her.

Dunn's narrative demands the abandonment of normality on the part of the reader, complete immersion into Olympia's topsy-turvy world. While the pleasure it provides is partially dependent on the perception of the difference of that world, and its shocking nature, there is also a sense in which Olympia invites the reader to share that world, to become, in the words of Browning's freaks, 'One of us'. In contemporary culture, the freakish self is no longer secret. In the late 1990s 'geek chic' was briefly elevated on the catwalk; an American teenage TV show called *Freaks and Geeks* was aired; celebrity culture often had the flavour of a sideshow, with Michael Jackson's increasingly bizarre physical appearance and lifestyle making headlines across the world; and genuine sideshows were revived in acts like the phenomenally successful Jim Rose Circus Sideshow, featuring one performer who lifted weights with his penis and another named the 'human pincushion'. In contrast to this celebration of the self-made freak, disability campaigners fought against a homogenizing mainstream culture that sought to 'correct' conditions it constructed as 'deformities'. Groups like the charity Changing Faces argued that they should not have to feel that their appearances are unacceptable and be forced into the position of having surgery so that their bodies conform to the 'norm'. While the courage of these campaigners and the validity of their project should not be diminished, it is perhaps enabled by a culture that prizes individuality, difference – in which people who would once have been constructed as freaks are able to struggle for acceptance, as the concept of freakishness is embraced by the culture at large.

AIDS and Viruses

AIDS, a disease passed through blood and other bodily fluids, and associated in the public mind with decadent lifestyles, has unsurprisingly been absorbed into contemporary Gothic modes of representation. In Francis Ford Coppola's film *Bram Stoker's Dracula* (1992), blood cells appeared in microscopic close-up on the screen, underlining the link between the mysterious disease of the blood attacking Lucy and its metaphorical relationship with our own contemporary blood disease. Elaine Showalter has highlighted the parallels between the current preoccupation with AIDS and the *fin-de-siècle* one with syphilis, although the texts she discusses are not specifically Gothic.[13] The parallel between one *fin-de-siècle* and another, however, is revisited in Will Self's *Dorian* (2002), an updating of Oscar Wilde's Gothic novel *The Picture of Dorian Gray* (1890) to the late twentieth century.

The Dorian of both novels is a different kind of monster to those discussed above. Dorian is freakish by means of his physical perfection, his freedom from the external indicators of ageing or corruption. His portrait, meanwhile, hidden away in the attic, takes on the outward signs of both his inward depravity and the natural ageing process. In Self's novel, the portrait is replaced by a video installation, *Cathode Narcissus*, in which a naked Dorian parades across nine screens. Wilde's cloaked references to homosexuality (the young men with whom Dorian chiefly associates have a tendency to commit suicide, or leave the country with their reputation in ruins) are overtly realized by Self in the gay scene of the 1980s and '90s, and the physical signs of depravity that register on the pictured Dorian's flesh reinterpreted as the ravages of drug addiction and AIDS. The virus's propensity to prey on the classically perfected bodies of gay men, remodelling them as grotesque, is figured in Gothic terms. Indeed, Henry Wotton, reimagined by Self as an upper-class heroin addict with the same penchant for outrageous witticisms as Wilde's dandy, declares: 'I feel gothic with disease – as if Cologne Cathedral were being shoved up my fundament.'[14] In a carnivalesque image, the godly medieval Gothic is brought down to earth in its gross juxtaposition with bodily orifices. Medieval architecture is reappropriated as a metaphor for bodily decay – a neat shift between the architectural and literary forms of Gothic outlined in the Introduction. However, the carnivalesque here seems to possess no power of renewal – it is an empty phrase, a blank witticism, subversive only in its refusal of the sanctimonious attitudes towards death expected by Henry's contemporaries.

Self's novel ends with two sharp twists absent from Wilde's earlier text. An Epilogue constructs a framing narrative, in which it is revealed that the story we have been reading is in fact the manuscript of a *roman-à-clef* written by one of its characters – Henry Wotton – while in the final throes of AIDS. The two existing copies are read and discussed by Henry's wife, Victoria, and Dorian himself – who does not seem to have killed himself at all, but is a healthy, successful entrepreneur at the head of the Gray Organisation, a fashionable media and design company. The narrative of *Dorian* is revealed to be the product of Henry's poisonous imagination, and of his jealousy of Dorian's superior achievements. Dorian judges that 'he'd become a twisted involution of homosexual self-hatred', conveniently side-stepping any potential criticisms Self might incur by presenting gay culture in a negative light.[15] *Dorian*, the Epilogue suggests, is the symptom of a certain kind of homosexual psychology, one steeped in shame and self-loathing, consonant perhaps with Wilde's historical context but anachronistic in the era of Gay Pride and the pink pound.

Self's second twist, however, restores the threat that had apparently been contained: Dorian begins to hear the voice of Henry Wotton, in a return of what the newly positive gay culture of the 1990s has repressed. Henry tells him that 'You've been living under an assumed identity, but your real name. And you're finding it *unheimlich*, if I'm not much mistaken.'[16] Henry presses the notion of the *unheimlich* or uncanny, Freud's notion of 'that class of the frightening which leads back to what is known of old and long familiar', comprising everything that 'ought to have remained secret and hidden but has come to light'.[17] What Dorian has hidden is, of course, Henry's manuscript, and all that it represents – the 'other' Dorian's debauchery, exploitation, narcissism and murder, but also Henry's black humour and iconoclasm. 'She had to die . . . because her name was Di', Henry's voice interjects facetiously in Dorian's head during the hysteria surrounding Princess Diana's death (a personal friend of Dorian's, naturally).[18] Self suggests that the attempt to divest the self of sin, of ageing, of fallibility represented both by Dorian's pact with his portrait and the super-Dorian of the Epilogue results in a brittle ego and multiple uncanny returns. Denying a dark side, shutting it away in the attic (as the Dorian of Self's Epilogue does to Henry's manuscript), is another kind of closeting. Contemporary gay identity is presented as thick with uncanny doubling, as its adherents try to achieve an identical model of beauty (represented by Dorian's appearance in *Cathode Narcissus*, pirated for TV advertisements and pop videos and 'spread through the virtual metabolism of the culture, like a digital virus').[19] Yet this quest for physical perfection is accompanied by the horrors of interchangeability, loss of identity, fragmentation of the body and the self, physical disgust, abjection. Attempting to escape Henry's voice through clubbing and drugs, Dorian finds himself back in the realm of the grotesque body. Henry taunts him: 'You're all completely interchangeable: cocks, arseholes, jeans, brains.

That joint you were in last night was like a swap shop at the end of the world, wouldn't you agree?'[20]

In a final return from the dead, Self's version of Dorian's nemesis, James Vane, the homeless gay drug addict Ginger, arrives to murder Dorian in a public lavatory. In a devastatingly Gothic finale, the transience of fashion is equated to that of human life, the horror of ignominious murder defused into surfaces: 'But by now he was also coming to terms with the fact that the beautiful new tie Ginger had just given him with his knife was a warm, sticky, fluid thing, and hardly likely to remain fashionable for very long at all.'[21]

Flesh and Spirit

The Picture of Dorian Gray is also echoed by Patrick McGrath's short story 'The Angel' (1988), more obliquely influenced by the spread of AIDS in the 1980s. This story is one of a number of recent Gothic works that appear to re-engage with religion, troubling the dichotomy between grotesque body and transcendent spirit and struggling towards the restoration of plenitude, depth, spiritual meaning – even faith. In this they echo what Graham Ward has called the 'turn to theology' in contemporary culture.[22] For Ward, one of the marked features of late capitalism has been a return to theological traditions as a reaction to the commodification of faith and 'the translation of values into market-developed lifestyles'. For Ward, however, Gothic plays into the production of religion as special effect, reintroducing 'Gnosticism into the cultural imagination: dark forces battle in apocalyptic fashion with the powers of light'.[23] This assertion is very broadly true, but only in the sense that it could be argued of the entire Western literary tradition. It takes a reductive view of both Gothic discourses and the place of religion within them. In fact, the battle between good and evil in Gothic texts has often been informed by specific theological arguments (the critique of Calvinism in James Hogg's Confessions of a Justified Sinner, for example; the fierce anti-Catholicism of Charlotte Bronte's *Villette*, 1853; or the Swedenborgianism of J. Sheridan Le Fanu's *Uncle Silas*, 1864). Victor Sage, in particular, has traced the specific theological controversies embodied in a 'Protestant Tradition' of horror writing.[24] Even in those exceptional texts that do confirm Ward's thesis – the battle of the Crew of Light with the arch-vampire in Bram Stoker's *Dracula* is perhaps the most obvious example – contemporary scholarship has profoundly problematized these divisions, interpreting Dracula as variously Semitic or a colonial other, and the Crew of Light as a homosocial, proto-Fascist alliance.[25] If Gothic as a set of discourses, as Horner and Zlosnik among others have argued, 'always concerns itself with boundaries and their instabilities', then it can be viewed as a place where clear divisions between good and evil, light and darkness, faith and disbelief are interrogated and blurred.[26] Prevailing motifs of Gothic such as heredity and contagion prohibit such dichotomies being enacted. McGrath's 'The Angel', as well as Rupert Wainwright's film *Stigmata* (1999) and the photographic works of Joel-Peter Witkin, provide excellent examples of this playing out of spiritual conflict.

Of the three texts I have selected here, 'The Angel' is the most obstinate in its refusal of transcendence. Bernard, a writer living in New York's Bowery district, befriends a camp elderly man named Harry Talboys, and persuades him to tell his story in the hope of finding material for a new book. It emerges that during the decadence of the Jazz Age Harry was in love with a dandyish, Dorian-like figure, Anson Havershaw, who claimed to be an angel. Prompted by Bernard's disbelief, Harry admits to him that he has been lying, but only about the identity of the angel – Harry and Anson are the same person. Harry then undresses to reveal that his lower torso has rotted almost entirely away, organs and bones exposed through gaping flesh, but explains that he cannot die. The moment of revelation is riven with ambivalence. On the one hand it professes to offer a kind of spiritual truth through the shock of physical horror; on the other, the vision is irremediably tainted, even bathetic: 'All I saw then was a young man standing in the corner of a shabby room watching an old man pull up his trousers.'[27] Bernard feels obligated to write Harry's story, but otherwise says that he now finds writing – and life – futile, and his only consolation is the knowledge that he can eventually die.

McGrath's short story offers a strange conjunction of spirit and flesh. Harry, the angel, is implicitly fallen, a 'lapsed' Catholic who follows a doctrine of self-expression akin to that described by William Blake's Devil in *The Marriage of Heaven and Hell* (*c.* 1790–93). Yet in secular twentieth-century New York, there is no heaven or hell against which his fall can be measured. As Harry states of his *alter ego*, Anson, 'Sin meant nothing to him; he was . . . pure soul in an age that did not believe in its existence.'[28] In the unbearable heat of mid-summer Manhattan, incense smoke barely disguising the stench of rotting flesh, the angel seems condemned to eternal life, trapped in a secular world in which the body is a prison. Yet this is at odds with his own doctrine that the body is sacred. Like Christ displaying his wounds, Harry offers queasy proof of his immortality through his physical incarnation. However, his version of the body as sacred is not one that would be recognized by the orthodox Church, as Bernard notes: 'what Catholic, after all, lapsed or otherwise, could ever believe the body was a temple in which nothing was unclean?'[29] Moreover, the notion of the flesh as sacred is contradicted by the sheer horror that the image of his physical decay produces. Bernard's glimpse of what lies beneath Harry's grubby surgical corset does not inspire faith but rather drains the meaning from his existence. 'This is what it means to be an angel, I remember thinking, in our times at least: eternal life burned in him while his body, his temple, crumbled about the flame.'[30] McGrath's angel is monstrous, but also pitiable, a 'Poor old man . . . lonely and shabby'.[31] He is more like Frankenstein's Creature than Christ, ambiguously monstrous and pitiable, given a voice and a history. The Creature, of course, also compared itself to Milton's fallen Lucifer. Harry's Blakeian doctrine of self-expression is mapped onto the emergence of a homosexual identity in the American Jazz

Age, but inevitably calls to mind the emergence of AIDS in the 1980s, when the story was written. McGrath's ultimate refusal to define Harry's rotting body as sacred or profane evokes the feeling of loathing and abjection apparently evoked by AIDS sufferers in their contemporaries, while complicating any easy moral judgement.

Rupert Wainwright's film *Stigmata* also sets up a continuity between the spiritual realm and the secular world, and it does so precisely through the body. The film is based on the premise that a worldly unbeliever begins to exhibit symptoms of the stigmata; it transpires that she is channelling a dead priest who wants to uncover a Vatican conspiracy to suppress a 'new' gospel, supposedly written by Christ. The film plays into the fascination with body modification emphasized by alternative culture in the 1990s, and enthusiastically embraced by Goth subculture, among others. Images of tattooing and body modification (the heroine Frankie has a navel tattoo and piercing) parallel those of Christian mortification; Frankie receives wounds to the feet while wearing platform shoes; a scene in a nightclub where she receives the Crown of Thorns recalls the chemically fuelled ecstatic states that revellers might more usually expect to achieve there. By presenting Frankie's wounds as beyond her control, however, *Stigmata* departs from the common interpretation of both self harm and body modification as performing a specific psychological function as a means for otherwise disempowered individuals to exert control over their environments. Paradoxically, Frankie's lack of faith makes her a martyr, since initially, at least, the stigmata offer her only torment, and not consolation. For Graham Ward, *Stigmata* is unusually radical in that it offers a figuration of a violent 'coming to belief' through visceral images of the gendered body, which function to undo the conventional body / soul dichotomy. The ending of the film, in which Frankie moves from suffering to grace, is for Ward a cop-out, in so far as it appears to reinstate, through the Gnostic Gospel of St Thomas, the division between the body and soul that the earlier portion of the film appears to challenge.

Patricia Arquette as Frankie in Rupert Wainwright's *Stigmata* (1999).

Ward's reading is stimulating, but in its over-simplification of the Gothic tradition overlooks some of the more obvious generic features of the film. In the Gothic novels of the eighteenth and early nineteenth centuries, written in the main by Protestants, there is a voyeuristic fascination with the exotic trappings of Catholicism: the mysteries of monasteries and nunneries, the terrors of the Inquisition, the dependence on visual icons. 'Good' Catholics, such as Ann Radcliffe's saintly M. St Aubert in *The Mysteries of Udolpho,* tend anachronistically to express values and beliefs consonant with those of the Protestant readership. *Stigmata* falls comfortably into this tradition. The Catholic Church is presented as a corrupt institution inimical to faith; the good priest regains his faith only to reject the Church (and, by implication, celibacy); the over-investment in religious objects (such as the stolen rosary that triggers Frankie's possession) is blurred into the superstition that they possess magical powers; the heretical gospel preaches a direct relationship with the divine unmediated by the Church that is more conducive to a Protestant viewpoint. What is striking about this film, as contemporary Gothic artefact, is that it ticks all the Gothic boxes – generic features are all present and correct – but that it ends neither with damnation nor with ambivalence, but with an affirmation of

81   GROTESQUE BODIES

faith. Marks on the surface of the body, a familiar Gothic motif, do not point back towards themselves, but index the ineffable mysteries of spiritual presence. The continual references to the smell of flowers pervading Frankie's apartment – the odour of sanctity – confound the audio-visual matrix of the cinema to suggest something the viewer cannot empirically access, only imagine. Moreover, the source of fear is not the Devil, as in most possession dramas, but rather God himself: inexplicable, mysterious and violent. It is almost as if, in a secular culture, the revival of religious feeling constitutes the ultimate return of the repressed. The cop-out is that we discover Frankie to be possessed by a Brazilian priest (contrarily reinstating the mediation of the Church at the very moment she experiences Christ), and not Jesus, after all – possession by the Godhead might be, after all, perceived as genuinely heretical.

The uneasy conjunction of spirit and flesh, sacred and profane, is also a defining feature of the work of the American photographer Joel-Peter Witkin. Witkin works in the same fairground tradition as Dunn: his subjects are fetishists, freaks and cadavers, placed in provocative tableaux, often referencing classic images of Renaissance art. His images question the truth-telling properties of the camera: unlike the nineteenth-century traditions of medical photographs or cartes-de-visites in which images of freaks were recorded as celebrities or as objects of scientific knowledge, Witkin's photographs resemble dreams and nightmares. Carefully staged with artificial backdrops and adulterated with marks and scratches before printing, they no longer possess the texture of celluloid but instead look like pages torn from arcane manuscripts. His models are not objectified but rather transfigured into potent and suggestively magical symbols of suffering and desire. Witkin restores the magic to monstrosity; his freaks are not tragic medical failures but wonders, marvels and portents. His work is troubling because it is not politically correct; it does not conform to contemporary notions of the positive representation of the differently abled. Many of Witkin's images, referencing as they do art historical tradition, in fact hark back to archaic modes of representation that in some cases might now be considered problematic. Nevertheless, each image is normally produced in close collaboration with its subject, and, according to Witkin, restores visibility to beings that Western culture would rather ignore. They are presented as spectacle, but the ambivalence of the image makes it difficult for the viewer to taxonomize, pity or otherwise appropriate the subject. Witkin's freaks are not domesticated; they are strange, disturbing and often difficult to look at. Here technology, in the form of photography, does not categorize or 'cure' the freak but enables its construction as unique, beautiful and utterly disquieting.

Witkin's frequent pastiching of classic art historical subjects or of specific paintings gives his work a quality of the uncanny: familiar images are revisited with a grotesque twist. *Las Meninas*, Witkin's version of Velázquez's famous painting, replaces the Infanta with a nine-year-old girl with vestigial legs, perched on top of a bell-shaped cage on wheels, the floor of which is spiked with nails. Like the Infanta in the original painting, the girl is simultaneously powerful and powerless. She is not enclosed by the cage but is immobile without it. The troubling nails distantly suggest Hans Christian Andersen's Little Mermaid, another marvellous freak, who achieved humanity at the price of being condemned to walk for the rest of her life on needles and pins. A subtle sense of threat thus underpins the image. The Infanta figure's eyes are screened by a light veil, another recurring motif in many of Witkin's works, along with the blindfold and the mask. The blocked gaze of his subjects paradoxically seems to make them more powerful, like visionaries or seers. Their refusal to return our gaze seems wilful and provocative, making us more self-conscious of our own act of looking. In *Las Meninas* seventeenth-century Catholic Spain is Gothicized in a way that parallels Gothic novels like *Melmoth the Wanderer* and *The Monk*, but which both acknowledges the props that support that particular construction and turns the gaze back on the viewer without jettisoning any of the image's sense of mystery and desire.

Joel-Peter Witkin, *Las Meninas New Mexico*, 1987, toned gelatin silver print photo.

Witkin's eschewal of realistic modes of representation in fact seems to point beyond the frame, to gesture towards transcendence of the flesh. Witkin has said that on a certain level, his pictures are all about himself, specifically about what he doesn't know. By deliberately seeking out the unknown, Witkin gestures towards the dark depths of the unconscious, but also towards the numinous, the mystical. Some of Witkin's figures are explicitly allegorical, like Prudence, looking forwards with the head of a beautiful young woman and backwards with the head of a corpse, or Abundance, a rich and gorgeous image of a limbless woman growing out of an urn, with a cornucopia of plenty poised on her head. Others, while rich with detail and incident, and therefore suggesting narratives, are almost impossible to summarize in words. They raise questions, provoking confusion and puzzlement rather than explanation: why is Leda a skeletal, polio-ravaged transvestite? Why does Beauty have three nipples?

Witkin is explicit in his debt to religious iconography, specifically the remnants of his Catholic upbringing. He imparts the quality of holy suffering to his subjects; they become contemporary martyrs and saints, bearing the weight of otherness. Thus, an image like *Un Santo Oscuro* translates its subject, a thalidomide casualty born without skin, hair, eyelids or limbs, into an icon of suffering, a body transcending the terrible continual pain of its condition (by extension, the human condition) to achieve spiritual presence. The grotesque is the gateway to the sublime.

Thus Witkin's work, while perhaps the most thoroughly and consistently Gothic of any contemporary artist, ultimately signals a change in Gothic sensibilities. While the performativity of the images, their claustrophobia, their pastiched historical content, their uncanniness and sheer horror, are long-established Gothic properties, their restoration of the spirit to the suffering flesh seems to point to a new kind of Gothic revival, a spirituality for our secular times.

Witkin's cadavers, unlike those of von Hagens, are not anonymous; they are replete with identity. They are unexpectedly real and unexpectedly full of life. The woman of *Interrupted Reading* sits to attention; the head of *Still Life*, its brain cavity blossoming with flowers, puns wittily on the art historical tradition, being both distinctly dead and disturbingly, suggestively, 'still alive'. These are bodies still in process, carnivalesque bodies. Fragmented, impaired, distorted, they never lack humour and are never less than human. They possess the texture of decaying flesh, not plastic; they retain the strangeness and terror of death while evoking queasy laughter. Both von Hagens and Witkin evoke the discourses of science: Von Hagens overtly, Witkin through the lineage of medical photography. Both seek in a way to transcend the body: von Hagens by preserving it and shaping it to his will, Witkin by imbuing the physical with the spiritual. Yet while von Hagens promises to show the 'reality' of the human body, his reality is an impoverished one, a body reduced to physical matter, stripped of meaning. Witkin, however, in his flight from realism, could be said to present the body in terms of mystical or spiritual 'truth'. This is the paradox of the body in contemporary Gothic: on the one hand it is simply one more feature in the procession of simulacra: endlessly repeated, endlessly manipulable. On the other its physicality is more present than ever before, as in the face of a decorporealized, information society we endlessly, obsessively assert that it breathes, that it dreams, that it feels pain.

CHAPTER THREE

Teen Demons

Gothic Teens

The body at the centre of many contemporary Gothic narratives is
definitively an adolescent one. This leads to further contradiction: on the
one hand, the physicality of the teen body is emphasized through the
visceral depredations of horror; on the other, teen Goth identities are
fashioned through performance and play, through the extraordinary
opportunities Gothic offers for dressing up. In the new teen Gothic, the
'surface trappings', the masks, veils and disguises that Eve Sedgwick
identifies as some of the most characteristic and daring features of Gothic,[1]
are of paramount importance. Contemporary teenage Gothic articulates a
tension between mainstream mass entertainment and a subcultural rebellion frequently expressed through style. As Rob Latham wrote of the
teenage vampire film *The Lost Boys* (1987): 'consumption . . . becomes for
teens both an avenue of self-expression and also of objectification in the
form of fashion. The result is an ambivalent dialectic of empowerment and
exploitation, in which teens are both consumers and consumed, vampires
and victims.'[2] Through clothing, the imperatives of consumerism and the
pleasures of performance intersect.

The Gothic heroine: a woodcut from the 1832 edition of Ann Radcliffe's *The Romance of the Forest*.

Gothic has always had a strong link with adolescence. While we should be cautious of applying a twentieth-century concept to pre-twentieth-century texts – ideas about what constitutes childhood are always culturally and historically specific – the heroines of the early Gothic novels by Ann Radcliffe and her contemporaries were almost invariably young women on the verge of adulthood, their threatened virginity the driving force of the plot. Even when, as in *The Mysteries of Udolpho* (1794), the villain shows rather more interest in the heroine's property than her person, her virginal status underlines her economic value, as marriageable commodity in herself and as legal executor of her inherited estates until the time they should pass to her husband. Constantly on guard against her potential violation, Radcliffe's Emily St Aubert occupies a liminal zone between the

Rousseau-esque innocence of childhood and the sexual maturity of marriage. It seems a long way between Emily St Aubert and a contemporary Gothic teenager like Buffy Summers, heroine of the film (1992) and TV series *Buffy the Vampire Slayer*, but historically distanced as they may be, Buffy and Emily clearly participate in the same tradition of representation. Ellen Moers argues in her landmark text *Literary Women* that the appeal of Gothic to women writers, at least, can be attributed in part to the outlet it offers for 'the savagery of girlhood'.[3] 'Girlhood' is here suggestively constructed along Gothic lines, as barbaric overthrow of 'proper', patriarchally sanctioned, adult femininity. There is a direct trajectory from Cathy's rebellion in *Wuthering Heights* (1847) to the modern teenage angst of the film *Ginger Snaps* (2000) or Rachel Klein's novel *The Moth Diaries* (2004).

According to Moers, the heroines of the earliest Gothic novels seemed intrepid for their historical context, enabling a female substitute for the more conventionally male-dominated picaresque. As Robert Kiely points out of Radcliffe's Emily, 'What we wonder about is not her virginity but her ingenuity under stress.'[4] *Buffy* may be a self-conscious critique of preceding models of Gothic femininity – in a Season Two episode, 'Hallowe'en', Buffy is turned into an eighteenth-century Gothic heroine by an enchanted costume, and predictably starts fainting and flirting before almost getting killed – but the series could not have existed without the Amelias and Emilies of Radcliffe's day, whose intrepid exploration of subterranean passages and vaults preceded those of their more witty and self-aware descendant.

What we might now think of as adolescents have also been consistently identified with the audience of Gothic. In his review of nineteen-year-old Matthew Lewis's *The Monk*, Samuel Taylor Coleridge reluctantly but dutifully warned against allowing the book to fall into the hands of children: 'the Monk is a romance, which if a parent saw in the hands of a son or daughter, he might reasonably turn pale'.[5] In *Northanger*

Abbey (1818), Jane Austen depicts seventeen-year-old Catherine Morland and her friend Isabella Thorpe infatuated with reading Gothic romances, constructing lists of new titles and rhapsodizing over their favourite – naturally, *The Mysteries of Udolpho*. Catherine, who 'from fifteen to seventeen . . . was in training for a heroine', becomes so involved in her reading matter that she begins to read her own life as if it were a Gothic novel, giving rise to a range of comic and not-so-comic misunderstandings.[6] Austen answers the accusations of contemporary critics, who condemned novel-reading for corrupting young women, either by introducing them to improper emotions (exemplified by Gregory's *A Father's Legacy to His Daughters*, 1774), or for making them silly and ineffectual in dealing with the realities of their lives (exemplified by Mary Wollstonecraft's *A Vindication of the Rights of Woman*, 1792). Catherine is duly shamed by her ludicrous supposition that Colonel Tilney has murdered his wife; yet, as feminist criticism has established, the patriarchal obsession with property that causes the heroine's downfall in so many Gothic novels does provide a valid model for understanding Tilney's tyrannical behaviour. Austen mounts a defence of her favourite novelists in the book, and in fact confirms Radcliffe's own moral point in *Udolpho*, that imagination should always be subordinated to reason. Nevertheless, the supposed power to corrupt impressionable youth possessed by Gothic texts has echoed down the centuries, culminating in the contemporary debate over the power of video nasties and 'Satanic' rock music.

During the Enlightenment, literature was supposed to have an educative moral function, one that was implicitly flouted by most Gothic texts (although part of Radcliffe's high reputation among her contemporaries was due to the fact that her novels *could* be read as moral in their lessons about the value of reason). Writers such as John and Anna Laetitia Aikin, influenced by Edmund Burke's theory of the Sublime, struggled to produce new means of explaining the purpose of tales of terror, suggesting that the imaginative stimulation elicited by visions of the supernatural 'awakens the mind', causing 'the expansion of its powers'.[7] It is possible to argue that many more recent horror films *do* in fact convey a very strong moral message. Numerous critics have pointed out that horror texts frequently uphold the dominant ideology, ending with the good rewarded and the bad punished. As the self-referential film *Scream* (1996) suggested, 'There are certain rules that one must abide by in order to survive a horror movie. For instance, number one: you can never have sex . . . Number two: you can never drink or do drugs – it's the sin factor . . . And number three – never, ever, ever, under any circumstances, say "I'll be right back".' Bad behaviour is consistently punished by the bogeyman: only the most wholesome teenagers go on to face the monster again in the sequel. (A witty reversal of this convention was provided by the film *Cherry Falls* of 2000, in which the serial killer murders only virginal teens, prompting sexual frenzy among high school students.) Yet the pleasure provided by the supernatural, violence and gore still provokes unease among censors. Even allowing for the moral ambiguity of a sizable minority of horror films, the very anxiety that the genre seems to elicit among certain groups of concerned adults seems to suggest that what happens in the film outweighs the closure, that the traditional good-triumphs-over-evil narrative is not enough to justify the depravities enacted en route. Nevertheless, audiences of the Gothic have always been asked to 'be pleased by what one dreads, take pleasure from distress, luxuriate in terror', as the critic Elizabeth Napier has put it.[8] The ambivalence, or as Napier describes it, instability, of this response is one of the most distinctive features of the genre. It perhaps contains an element of masochism but also, more significantly, what Chris Baldick has referred to as a 'homeopathic' remedy to anxiety: a little bit of what scares you, particularly in a form that is clearly fictional and removed from real life, actually allows you safely and temporarily to indulge and therefore ward off feelings of fear.[9] Contemporary Western culture constructs adolescence as a time of particular anxiety, a transitional phase between childhood 'innocence' and adult 'knowledge'. Within this framework,

Gothic narratives seem to offer one particular strategy for negotiating the terrors of the 'unknown'.

Subcultural Style

The teenager proper was brought into being by post-war consumer culture, eager to identify and target a new demographic. The young women on the verge of sexual maturity that predominate in many eighteenth- and nine-teenth-century narratives are realized in contemporary Gothic as modern teenagers, complete with all the anxieties and desires that twentieth- and twenty-first-century Western culture imputes to adolescence. The churning out of teen-oriented Gothic, from pre-teen popular fiction such as the *Goosebumps* series to 18-certificate horror films set in American high

A contemporary interpretation of the Gothic heroine, at Whitby Gothic Weekend, April 2005.

Contemporary Goth, as seen at Whitby Gothic Weekend in 2005: a combination of faux-period, Punk and fetish styles.

schools, is evidence of the drive of a commercial marketing machine that views teenagers as a valuable resource to be tapped for ready cash. In distinction to this, an autonomous youth culture has developed since the late 1970s that derives its aesthetic from the Gothic literary and cinematic tradition and is relatively resistant to mainstream consumerism and advertising, 'Goth', as this subculture has become known, is by no means restricted to teenagers and is largely represented in the mass media, even within horror films themselves, as a negative stereotype (a corrective to this is provided by the sequel to the Blair Witch movie, *Book of Shadows*, in which the Goth girl is the only relatively sympathetic character). Nevertheless, the association of teenagers with Gothic often falls back on Goth subculture in popular perception, a notion I wish both to challenge and discuss.

Goth is a controversial and frequently contested term. Here, I take it to mean that youth subculture that derives its visual style and preoccupations from Gothic literary and cinematic tradition, which first emerged in Britain in the late 1970s, but which, like many youth movements, spread quickly across the Atlantic and beyond. Goth encompasses a diverse set of visual styles and subcultural practices that commentators should beware of homogenizing, but which at the same time *are* frequently homogenized and subjected to stereotype by both mainstream and alternative media. One characteristic set of media responses labels the subculture as comically pretentious, self-indulgent and middle-class. Johnny Cigarettes, in the now-defunct British music magazine *Vox*, wrote: 'a nice, totally unspectacular upbringing is just not interesting enough, so [Goths] have to get into lots of pretend-nasty stuff, pretend to be tortured and self-destructive, and slack around on the dole all day'.[10] Ellen Barry, writing in the *Boston Phoenix*, made a similar point more sympathetically: 'From the very beginning, goth [sic] spoke to the particular world-weariness of the middle-class adolescent. Its followers were alienated by their parents, who were prosperous, and by their classmates, who were preppy, and by the culture at large, which was cheerful . . . Who can blame them for reading too much Keats?'[11] An article published in *The Guardian* in 2006 noted the number of ex-Goths who end up in high-flying professions, putting this down to the fact that the subculture tends to attract more intellectual teenagers.[12] Interestingly, this response is frequently used to parody the subculture sympathetically from within, as in Jhonen Vasquez's satirical 'Anne Gwish' cartoon strip or Serena Valentino's affectionately arch *Gloom Cookie* comic. The tabloid media and the American Christian far right, on the other hand, tend to present a more sensational set of associations between Goth, Satanism, sado-masochism and vampire activities.

Clothing is essential to Goth subculture: Goth can be broadly categorized as what Dick Hebdige labels a 'spectacular' subculture, one that seeks to enact symbolic resistance through a controversial and clearly recognizable

Goth style icon Siouxsie Sioux, 1983.

visual style.[13] Although other aspects of the subculture – music, shared interest in particular books and films, activities such as clubbing – are crucial in the formation of Goth identities, visual appearance is perhaps its most definitive feature. Goth style has many permutations, varying both regionally and according to musical taste (in Australia, many Goths sport parasols to preserve their pale complexions). To outsiders, however, it appears fairly consistent, with a predilection for black clothing in a combination of faux-period, Punk and fetish styles, elaborate jewellery, 'vamp' make-up for both sexes, and dyed hair, also frequently black. Style icons include, among many others, Peter Murphy and Daniel Ash of Bauhaus, Siouxsie Sioux of Siouxsie and the Banshees, Andrew Eldritch and Patricia Morrison of The Sisters of Mercy, Nick Cave of The Birthday Party and the Bad Seeds, and, latterly, Marilyn Manson – although dispute rages among fans over whether Manson's commercial heavy metal can truly be considered 'Goth'.

The Dresden Dolls' Gothic-tinged 'Brechtian Punk Cabaret', 2006.

Gothic Country: The Handsome Family, 2003.

Music, too, is crucial to defining Goth subcultural identity. From the late 1970s, when bands like Bauhaus, Siouxsie and the Banshees and the Birthday Party began to take Punk in a darker direction, through the mainstream chart success of The Sisters of Mercy, The Mission and The Cure in the 1980s, to the harder 'Industrial' sound of Ministry and Nine Inch Nails in the 1990s, Goth has evolved in a number of different directions. While it may be possible to identify a core sound, distinguished by doomy lyrics, melodramatically deep or atmospherically ethereal vocals, heavy bass-lines and a post-Punk sensibility, what has been defined as Goth by fans has always been fairly flexible, taking in a wide range of musical styles. In practice, both Goth and alternative labels such as 'Darkwave' are mutable and contested, means of mapping loose affiliations of taste rather than of delivering identity. This is complicated by the fact that many Goth musicians – including most of those cited above – frequently refuse to identify themselves with the Goth scene, dissociate themselves from the term. In the twenty-first century, Goth has become increasingly diffuse, with most bands sufficiently underground never to register with the mainstream media. Some of the most interesting contemporary Gothic music arises, as in the literary context, from the cross-fertilization of genres. The Dresden Dolls, for example, perform Punky, Gothically inflected cabaret, their song 'Girl Anachronism' (2003) tracing a damaged life right back to delivery by Caesarean section. In contrast, The Handsome Family write Gothic Country and Western, albums like *Through the Trees* (1998), *Singing Bones* (2003) and *Last Days of Wonder* (2006) assembling macabre and sometimes bizarre tales of loneliness, haunting and death. The mid-1990s genre of 'Trip Hop', while not associated with Goth subculture, elicited tracks of aural unease by bands such as Portishead and Tricky that use sampling and distortion to create claustrophobic, haunted auditory space. Meanwhile, Indie bands such as Bloc Party, The Rapture, The Violets and The Horrors recycle Goth influences from the 1980s in a hip new context. The likes of Nick Cave, The Cure and Siouxsie Sioux (in a Banshees side project, The Creatures) are still releasing records, of course, but, now approaching their fifties, they seem increasingly institutionalized.

Goth as a musical style is perhaps most clearly united through a sense of performativity, of dressing up. What leads a band to be labelled Goth (as opposed to Gothic in the more literary sense) is ultimately usually visual style. It is also clothing that most securely links Goth subculture with the Gothic literary tradition. According to Eve Sedgwick, 'surface' features of Gothic fiction such as veils, masks and disguises are frequently where the most striking Gothic effects occur.[14] The Gothic fakery and theatricality described in chapter One are translated in this context into concepts of costume and masquerade. As I have argued recently in *Fashioning Gothic Bodies*, 'Goth . . . represents another manifestation of the Gothic preoccupation with clothes.'[15] In this book, I suggest that the cultural associations between fashion and femininity typically function to gender Goth feminine, despite the higher visibility of men in the Goth music scene. Teen Gothic frequently redeploys this association through its representation of teenage girls both in and out of Goth costume.

Grrrl Power

Not all of the contemporary associations between Gothic and teenagers can be credited to Goth. There are a number of youth cultural influences that have contributed to the rise of *Buffy*, *Scream* and their numerous imitators and spin-offs. One of these is the increasing prominence of teenage girls within popular culture. While horror films were, in the 1970s and '80s, regarded as primarily attracting teenage boys (an extension of a wider Hollywood identification of its audience with male teens), the acknowledgement of a significant female audience for the genre has played a part in the development of new kinds of Gothic heroines. Carol Clover's seminal work *Men, Women and Chainsaws* argued that the slasher film offers an inevitably compromised but potentially progressive figure: the 'Final Girl', the female protagonist who

> (1) undergoes agonizing trials, and (2) virtually or actually destroys the antagonist and saves herself. By the lights of folk tradition she is not a heroine, for whom phase 1 consists in being saved by someone else, but a hero, who rises to the occasion and defeats the adversary with his own wit and hands.[16]

While in the films Clover discusses the Final Girl's apparent subversiveness is mitigated by her acting as a boy in disguise, enabling trans-gender identification, or by her subjection to voyeuristic sadism, contemporary reworkings of the archetype increasingly stress its positive, feminist potential. The development of the central character over seven seasons of *Buffy the Vampire Slayer*, for example, allows her to develop an emotional and sexual identity that complicates any notion of her as an object of voyeurism or boy in disguise; moreover, the series' splicing of horror with teen soap opera and romance confuses the generic signals, suggestively feminizing a genre hitherto associated with a masculine audience. Clover ignores, too, the Final Girl's origin in the heroine of the eighteenth-century Gothic novel, so frequently positioned as being read and written by women.

This reworking of the 'Final Girl' reflects a wider cultural shift. *The phrase of the mid-1990s was 'Girl Power': initially the title of an album by the pop-Punk girl band Shampoo, it was appropriated by the Spice Girls and turned into a global slogan. 'Girl Power' was a kind of oxymoron: girls (women without the authority of age and experience) are a social group consistently constructed as powerless throughout the recent history of Western culture. As the cultural theorists Angela McRobbie and Jenny Garber note, until recently studies of youth subcultures have tended to ignore girls, because social constraints have tended to make them less visible in street-oriented subcultures than their male counterparts.[17] Their solution, writing in the 1970s, is to examine the 'teenybopper' culture that teenage girls enjoy in the privacy of their bedrooms. They argue that this culture has been denigrated because it is definitively commercial, promoted through heavily targeted pop records and magazines. This culture lacks the credibility of, say, the delinquent street gangs that feature in numerous sociological studies. Nevertheless, it is often the only culture available to young women who suffer more restrictions on their activities than their male peers; it allows them an autonomous space in which to express themselves, and is immensely significant to the girls themselves in defining their subjectivities.

In the early twenty-first century, teenybopper culture still exists, although it is as likely to be directed at gay men or pre-teens as it is at teenage girls. The enormous success of Take That, the Spice Girls and all the boy and girl bands that followed in their wake is testament to that. With the Spice Girls, it was discovered that feminism could be sugar-coated and marketed to twelve-year-olds, with momentous effects. The culture of teenage girls has, in effect, become central to mainstream media culture as a whole. On the other hand, the bedroom subcultures that McRobbie and Garber described re-emerged in a radicalized, anti-commercial form as Riot Grrrl, a girl-oriented subculture with a DIY ethic that focused on the foregrounding of female experience through fanzines, websites and post-Punk music. Riot Grrrl – gritty, raw and uncompromising – was the antithesis of teenybopper, although it may have germinated from similar female teenage experiences. It genuinely engaged with feminism and totally rejected the commercialism of mainstream pop – as a memorable lyric from the influential British group Huggy Bear declared: 'They wanna make a T-shirt out of your dreams.'[18] However, both movements accorded girls power of a kind: the power to express oneself on the one hand, the power of the consumer on the other. Both of these forms of power were arguably illusory: Riot Grrrl's policy of mainstream media boycott ultimately guaranteed its insularity, while the power to consume is arguably no power at all. In both its counter-cultural and commercial forms, however, girl power was top of the agenda.

As the 1990s drew to a close, more and more films and television programmes began to appear in which girls did possess power, frequently of a supernatural nature. Most prominent of these was *Buffy the Vampire Slayer*, in which the eponymous heroine is the 'Chosen One', a teenage girl possessing superhuman fighting and self-healing abilities, with which she constantly battles to save the world from the vampire and demon hordes seeking to exploit it. Similar programmes included *Charmed* (1998–2006), which follows the exploits of three sisters who are witches (one sister being replaced by a cousin in later series), and *Sabrina the Teenage Witch* (1996–2003), a spin-off from a film of the same name. The popularity of girl witches in the media was matched by a surge of interest in Wicca, reportedly the fastest growing religion in twenty-first-century America: books such as Silver Ravenwolf's *Teen Witch* (1998) enable their young audience to learn the rudiments of magic first-hand. Such books stress self-empowerment as much as they do magical powers: the version of spirituality they offer is heavily filtered through the language of self-help manuals and bolstered by the need for an impressive range of material accessories, from candles and crystals to robes and ritual equipment. Most books stress the equal efficacy of cheap alternatives, but magical supplies sustain a substantial industry nevertheless. As Diane Purkiss has observed, 'The discourses of self-improvement are very dominant here; the self constructed is the familiar self of late capitalism, the striving, upwardly mobile self who controls her own destiny.'[19] For Purkiss, the spells offered in such guidebooks are for the most part vague, tame, solipsistic and valorize retrogressive models of femininity as domestic, defensive and 'good'. There is little to upset any but the most devoutly religious parents in these life manuals for teenagers with an alternative bent. A BBC documentary screened in 2002 showed a group of teenage Wiccans performing a spell to help one of them raise the money to buy a longed-for Versace jacket.[20] In sharp contrast, 'bad' media witches such as Nancy in the teenage film *The Craft* (1996) or Dark Willow in Season Six of *Buffy the Vampire Slayer* vividly express rage, desire and a hunger for power in a way that tends to exceed its framing by a critical viewpoint and plot resolution in favour of 'good' uses of magic (I will return to this later). None of this should necessarily be read as representative of wider Wiccan culture and beliefs, but rather to suggest that its increasing popularization and commercialization during the 1990s both reflected and reinforced the association of teenagers with the occult.

The New Teen Gothic

The characteristic feature of teen Gothic in the 1970s and '80s was loss of control: the world becomes turned upside down as an external force takes over, haunting or possessing the teenagers at the centre of the narrative. The teenagers are victims, even when they survive for the sequel, struggling to outwit the supernatural forces ranged against them and to regain control of their world. Nancy in *A Nightmare on Elm Street* (1984) and Laurie in *Hallowe'en* (1978) are terrorized by their aggressors and outwit them only after long periods in which their bodies are placed under threat. In *The Exorcist* (1973), the pre-pubescent Regan is not herself a demonic supernatural force but is possessed by one. In the teen Gothic of the 1990s and beyond, the teenagers seem to have taken control of the narrative. On the one hand they possess special powers that enable them to combat the forces of the evil, like Buffy Summers; on the other they may themselves be the monsters, like the vampire Nothing in Poppy Z. Brite's novel *Lost Souls* (1992), the murderous teenage horror aficionados of *Scream* or the were-wolf Ginger of *Ginger Snaps*. While old-fashioned 'threatened teen' movies are still plentiful (*I Know What You Did Last Summer*, *Jeepers Creepers*, even *The Blair Witch Project*), there is a knowingness about these films that sets them apart from their predecessors. The new teen Gothic is more *Northanger Abbey* than *The Mysteries of Udolpho* in that both characters and audience are aware of the conventions, and subject them to critical scrutiny and ironic investigation.

In the new teen Gothic, furthermore, the outsider takes on a new and different role. As argued in the previous chapter, a recurrent feature of contemporary Gothic is sympathy for the monster: those conventionally represented as 'other' are placed at the centre of the narrative and made a point of identification for the reader or viewer. In the teen Gothic of the 1990s a similar manoeuvre takes place: the freaks and geeks are no longer pushed to the edges of the narrative but become the protagonists. The social structure of the American teen movie of the 1980s, in which a form of social apartheid exists between jocks and prom queens on the one hand and geeks and misfits on the other, forms the template for much contemporary teen Gothic. Whereas in movies of the 1980s such as *Sixteen Candles*

(1985), *Pretty in Pink* (1986) and *The Breakfast Club* (1985) the socially marginalized characters are invariably integrated with their peers by the end of the narrative, in contemporary teen Gothic marginalization is often celebrated. In the TV series of *Buffy the Vampire Slayer*, Buffy crosses the divide in the opposite direction, leaving behind her vacuous cheerleading past when she embraces her role as the Slayer and throwing in her lot with bookish Willow and class clown Xander. Although all three characters undergo shifts in social status over the course of the series, none ever becomes popular as such; their everlasting task of ridding the world of vampires and demons isolates them from their peers and allows them to retain their geeky cool.

The focus on the outsider, traditionally a feature of what has been called 'male' Gothic, which focuses on the psychology of the villain rather than heroine, has also enabled a teen Gothic more oriented towards masculinity, reinterpreting the theme of social alienation with relish. Johnny Depp's performance as the eponymous hero of Tim Burton's *Edward Scissorhands* (1990) forms the prototype: a fairy-tale version of Frankenstein's Creature, Edward's outward monstrosity serves as a light-ning-rod for the inward monstrosity of suburban America. Richard Kelly's *Donnie Darko* (2001) depicts its hero ambiguously haunted by an evil, giant rabbit named Frank, replaying the theme of the demonic double familiar from Hogg's *The Private Memoirs and Confessions of a Justified Sinner* or Stevenson's *Strange Case of Dr Jekyll and Mr Hyde* within a high school context. Donnie's troubled modern adolescence is thus mapped back onto earlier models of Gothic masculinity, producing an uncannily resonant figure. Pre-empting the preoccupation with delinquent youth in 'hoodies', Donnie draws up his hood when under Frank's influence, like a Grim Reaper in casual clothing. The Director's Cut of the film played down the notion of the double, removing the psychological ambiguity of the earlier release by stressing that Frank was an otherworldly visitor, and thus tended to de-Gothicize it: Donnie is not himself a monster, simply visited by one.

The crucial precedent for the new teen Gothic is *Carrie* (1976), the film based on the Stephen King novel of the same name. In this film, a bullied teenager takes bloody revenge on her oppressors with her telekinetic powers. Carrie is a victim, oppressed by her fanatical mother and casually cruel classmates, but she is also a monster, who slaughters almost all her high school companions. She is not the 'good girl' represented by Jamie Lee Curtis's Laurie in *Hallowe'en*. However, she is not straightforwardly 'evil' either. As Gregory A. Waller suggests, Carrie represents a particular kind of horror monster who is outside or beyond conventional morality.[21] Significantly, she is also on the brink of adolescence: the opening sequence sees her experience the onset of menstruation in the school's communal showers. This disturbing scene seems evocative on a variety of levels, and not only the obvious one that associates telekinetic powers with adolescent girls. Donald Campbell argues that teenagers are so attracted to horror movies because the morphing bodies shown on screen echo their own. As David Punter explains,

> [T]he root of the attraction of horror movies for adolescents lies less in bloody murder than in a prevailing atmosphere of disgust which provides duplicate images for the adolescent's disgust with the changes in his or her own emerging body, from acne to menstruation. The body, we might say, is always rising up against the adolescent, a bloody, half-formed body, in which things which should be kept inside are always pressing to and out of the surface, while the things which beg for outer attention – emotions, self-images – have no means of outlet and must be kept down in an apparently permanent state of tension.[22]

A provocative if rather essentialist idea, this overlooks the way that the adolescent passion for horror can also constitute a very conscious rebellion against parentally or societally 'approved' reading or viewing matter.

These two ideas are brought together by *Ginger Snaps*. On the one hand the eponymous Ginger and her sister Bridget, or 'B', enact a conscious rebellion against their parents and teachers by deliberately engaging with horror imagery. In the opening sequences of the film, the sisters are shown staging a series of photographs in which they are the victims of bloody and frequently improbable deaths, in order to complete a school assignment. The images themselves, which play during the title credits, are both hilarious and shocking, mocking horror film expectations (Ginger is shown impaled on a white picket fence before the camera cuts to her sister holding a camera and complaining 'too much blood!'). They suggest that the sisters are in control of their world, and that horror can be used performatively as a means of forging individual identity and transmuting adolescent anxiety into play.

On the other hand, the film follows Donald Campbell's premise to the letter: Ginger is bitten by a werewolf at the onset of menstruation, and the links between becoming an adolescent and becoming a monster are made quite literally. In a comic scene in the school nurse's office, the revelation that Ginger is experiencing pain and growing hair where none existed before is dismissed as entirely normal. She defends her behaviour to her sister by arguing 'I just got my period, OK? Now I've got weird hairs, so what! That means I've got hormones, and they may make me butt-ugly, but they don't make me a monster.' As Ginger discovers herself growing a tail, she also develops an appetite for sex, drugs and violence. The more prosaic dangers of unprotected sex are also alluded to as Ginger passes the werewolf virus to a sexual partner after failing to use a condom. A 'menstruation movie' in the tradition of *Carrie*, *Ginger Snaps* demonstrates a distinctive shift in sensibilities from Carrie's victim-turned-avenger.

The tone of *Ginger Snaps* is difficult to ascertain, which is partly what makes it such a successful film. In her conversion to a werewolf, Ginger is both sexy and sympathetic. Like Carrie, she uses her powers to avenge herself on the school bullies, although with more bathetic results (after hiding the body of the school bitch in the ice chest, Ginger and her sister Bridget find it so frozen that they are forced to chisel it out with a screwdriver, breaking off several fingers in the process). Unlike Carrie, she is never a victim. Her family, while annoyingly dysfunctional, are nevertheless relatively ordinary, and even before her lycanthropic conversion Ginger is easily able to defend herself and her sister both physically and verbally at school. Rather, she articulates a certain feminine adolescent rage usually repressed in teen movies. Ginger is not a nice girl, in the manner of most horror-film heroines. She recognizes a world in which only certain models of femininity are permitted and is prepared to trade on that: concealing one of her crimes, she tells Bridget: 'No-one ever thinks chicks do shit like this. Trust me – a girl can only be a slut, a bitch, a tease, or the virgin next-door. We'll just coast on how the world works.' She refuses to play by the rules or fit into the roles expected of her. Provoked by a comically over-defensive sexual partner who asks 'Who's the guy here?', Ginger replies: 'Who's the fucking *guy* here? . . . You're fucking hilarious cave-boy!' Yet her monstrosity is unsustainable: increasingly out of control, and increasingly unrecognizable as human, she must die at the end of the film. The metaphor collapses as Ginger loses her grip on her humanity and becomes entirely other, a grotesque, bestial creature. While the film seems ultimately to capitulate to the demands of the genre, which requires a bloody stalk-and-slash sequence at the end of the film culminating in the monster's destruction, Ginger's glorious and spectacular expression of rage seems to transcend the film's conservative closure. Ginger is no threatened teen, but rather a teenaged threat.

This shift from the threatened teen to the teen as threat runs through contemporary teen Gothic. Teenagers themselves are now as likely to be the source of horror as the victim of it. This seems to reflect a two-edged trajectory: on the one hand teenagers, particularly girls, are being presented as more powerful and in control of their lives; on the other, teen Gothic capitalizes on real-life moral panics about teenage violence, such as the Columbine High School Massacre in 1999.

Marilyn Manson, 2005: media folk devil or canny self-publicist?

Teenage Threats

The Columbine Massacre took place on 20 April – Hitler's birthday. The perpetrators, Eric Harris and Dylan Klebold, came from comfortable middle-class backgrounds in the suburbs of Denver, Colorado. Between them, they shot and killed twelve fellow students and a teacher at their high school, injuring numerous others, before turning their guns on themselves. The media almost immediately seized on the fact that Harris and Klebold characteristically wore black trench coats and purportedly listened to Industrial metal bands like KMFDM. They were labelled as Goths, and their violence attributed to a youth culture preoccupied with the morbid and macabre. The self-styled 'Antichrist Superstar' Marilyn Manson, who was due to play in Denver shortly after the event, was made a media scapegoat for the crimes, as the most commercially successful and instantly recognizable 'face' of a youth subculture preoccupied with decadence, dissent and death. His 'Satanic' influence was evoked as a corrupting agent in an argument uncannily similar to that of *fin-de-siècle* eugenicist Max Nordau, who proposed in his bestseller *Degeneration* (1891–2) that the Decadent artist could cause the race to decline by transmitting his enervating influence to impressionable audiences.[23] Regardless of whether Harris and Klebold actually listened to or were particular fans of Manson's music, Manson's deliberate media strategy of baiting right-wing Christian America meant that he was already in place as a convenient folk devil. (Interestingly, the British music weekly *New Musical Express* commented in 2004 that Manson's 'standing as a national hate figure . . . lasted only two years, demolished along with the first twin tower'.)[24]

Manson's own response to the events at Columbine was sensitive and intelligent: questioned by Michael Moore in the documentary *Bowling For Columbine* (2002) about what he would say to the murderers, he responded: 'I wouldn't say a single word to them, I would listen to what

'Satanic' killer Manuela Ruda in court, 2002.

they have to say – and that's what no-one did.' Those individuals who considered themselves Goths, or as sympathetic to Goth subculture, were alarmed by the media witch-hunt, and a spate of articles appeared in the broadsheets and alternative press, and on the Internet, defending Goth and distancing Harris and Klebold from the subculture. Characteristically, writers stressed the peaceful disposition of most Goths, their interest in literature and culture, the importance of fantasy, and the tenuousness of any connection with Satanist or, as in the more sensationalist accusations, neo-Nazi groups. Goths were usually the ones persecuted in high school, they pointed out; the real danger of media demonization was that more teenagers would be alienated from and victimized by their peers. The Columbine murders had reversed the pattern of the usual high school narrative, where the 'popular' students persecute the geeks. Harris's and Klebold's crimes caught the public imagination at least partly because they reproduced the outsider's revenge against the wholesome American world of jocks and cheerleaders that had been routinely fictionalized in Hollywood cinema for decades.

Harris and Klebold were not the only criminals to be associated in the media with Gothic discourses. Manuela and Daniel Ruda, the 'Vampire Killers of West Germany', were convicted in 2002 of murdering one of Daniel's colleagues as part of a Satanic ritual. Daniel and Manuela apparently believed that they were vampires, and Manuela's spectacular Goth style ensured that she made newspaper front pages across the world. The British media focused on the years that Manuela spent on London's underground Goth scene, and again came to sensational conclusions about how teenagers could be corrupted by their engagement with Goth subculture.

The standard arguments that are always made in relation to accusations of media influence on criminals all apply here: perhaps individuals with dark tendencies are drawn to and distort horror films/rock music/subcultures rather than being corrupted by them; making folk devils out of rock stars or subcultures distracts attention from underlying social problems; if individuals are that way inclined they will find something to inspire their actions no matter what (such as Charles Manson's appropriation of the Beatles). However, we can also see more specifically Gothic narratives at work. Historically, Gothic has been about theatricality, camp, dressing up – Horace Walpole's arm-length gloves as he came to greet his visitors at Strawberry Hill, Richard Mansfield's flamboyant performance on the nineteenth-century London stage as both Dr Jekyll *and* Mr Hyde, the rock singer Siouxsie Sioux's elaborate costumes. What is intended as performative fantasy, however, does have the potential to be misinterpreted by the audience as real. Mansfield's performance was allegedly so convincing that he was briefly considered as a suspect for the Jack the Ripper murders. More recently, in a kind of reprise of this fallacy, Patricia Cornwell has notoriously read the Post-Impressionist artist Walter Sickert's fascination with Jack the Ripper as proof that he *was* Jack the

Ripper.[25] This could be regarded as neglecting a fundamental difference between art and life (or fiction and criminal procedure), or merely as a lack of imagination. A more worrying trend in contemporary Gothic, however, is the collapse of performance into reality, the jettisoning of artifice for authenticity. Thus for Manuela Ruda, the fantasy re-enactment of being a vampire was not sufficient; she believed she really was a vampire, and must reify that belief with the appropriate acts. Goth performativity clashed with the striving for 'authenticity' inherent to subcultural identity: an interest in vampires and a taste for Gothic style moved beyond performance and play to over-identification. The Rudas no longer sought to ward off the threat but instead to become the threat.

The drive to turn Gothic artifice into reality bedevils teen Gothic. On the one hand, it creates the kind of tabloid outrage that proclaims Marilyn Manson as the most dangerous man in America – a label he is happy to embrace, since it is good for business, but which has been greeted with ridicule by the more prosaic British music press. On the other hand, a nostalgic longing for fixed identity imbues youth culture with a new essentialism. As Katherine Ramsland demonstrates in *Piercing the Darkness* (1999), in the 1990s a new subculture emerged in America that is based on vampirism and that also dissociates itself quite stridently from Goth. Although the scene incorporates a range of beliefs regarding vampirism and vampire identity, the hardcore members of the subculture refer to themselves as Real Vampyres and are derogatory about wannabes, role-players and, of course, Goths. The implication is that these lesser groups simply like dressing up – pretending – while the Real Vampyres possess an authentic vampire identity, more often than not affirmed by blood-drinking practices. This new essentialism is reflected in Poppy Z. Brite's vampire novel, *Lost Souls* (1992), in which the teenage vampire Nothing is distanced from and implicitly superior to his Goth friends, and in which his vampiric identity is the cause of his social alienation rather than an effect.[26] In other words he is depressed because he is really a vampire, not simply interested in vampires because he is depressed. This corresponds to a question raised by one of Ramsland's interviewees: 'Let's examine motives. When did you first get your craving for blood . . . ? Was it after you became a fan of vampire fiction?'[27] For Nothing, the identity emphatically precedes cultural knowledge.

Despite their insistence on their own authenticity, however, the Real Vampyres seem excessively preoccupied with dressing the part. The problem of what to wear as a vampire is highlighted by Ramsland's exposé of the American vampire scene. Ramsland, trained in clinical psychology and philosophy but perhaps best known as Anne Rice's biographer, decided to investigate vampire subculture following the mysterious disappearance of a journalist, Susan Walsh, who had been researching the scene. The most remarkable thing about her ensuing discoveries is how boring they are: most of the fantasies and life-stories divulged by the 'Real Vampyres' she encounters are inevitably rather repetitive. Perhaps the most interesting aspect of the narrative is her own struggles with the dress codes at the vampire club nights and fetish balls she is required to attend 'undercover'. At her first vampire club, the Long Black Veil, she states: 'The requested attire was "Dark Fetish, Goth, Arthurian, Edwardian, Vampire, Rubber, or Victorian." I wore black.'[28] Later on, about to be fitted with her first pair of fangs, she encounters three young people sporting piercings and tattoos, and subsequently remarks:

> They let me pass, but I was aware how strange I looked. I had on an ordinary blouse and skirt – at least the skirt was black! – and my hair lacked frizz, spikes, or any other type of the exotic ornamentation I saw all around on the street below. So did my face. I felt utterly conspicuous.[29]

Ramsland gradually acquires the visual techniques of vampirism and is able to converse with the most elusive members of the scene. Attending a Vampire Ball in New York, dressed for the part 'with a long black gypsy wig, fangs, black velvet gloves, velvet lace-up boots . . . a black velvet dress, and a bright red velvet hooded opera cloak with gold chains', plus the requisite make-up, she is proud to note that 'I wasn't sure anyone would know me. (They didn't).'[30] Again, however, the most striking thing about the appearance of the vampires she meets is its repetitiveness. One or two do dress 'straight', but most conform to the Goth or fetish look, despite their keenness to dissociate themselves from Goths. Virtually all of them wear black, adhering to literary and cinematic tradition, and evoking associations with the hours of darkness, the demonic and the funereal. This is a convention that is reiterated by representations of vampires on screen, which rarely depart from a Goth look. Goth, it seems, has become visual shorthand for vampirism; we want our vampires to be readily identifiable, to conform to a set sartorial code. Even *Buffy*, the vampire narrative most playful with convention and intolerant of cliché, has Goth vampires. And it is precisely in its use of Goth clothing that *Buffy* struggles most with the performance / authenticity dichotomy.

Buffy and Goth

Buffy the Vampire Slayer has received an unprecedented level of critical and academic attention compared to previous television shows, partly for the sophistication of its witty, complex, densely intertextual narratives, and partly because its story of an ordinary Californian teenager chosen to save the world from the Forces of Darkness apparently captured the imagination of her generation. Although at the time of writing it is still less than a decade since the series began, it has already generated a formidable academic industry. *Buffy* is the text that perhaps more than any other embodies the possibilities of contemporary Gothic: not only does it constantly interrogate the stories and generic conventions from which it springs (the double, in 'Doppelgangland'; the Frankenstein myth in Season Four; the greatest vampire of them all in 'Buffy vs. Dracula'), but it also plays games with other genres (the musical, in 'Once More With Feeling'; the docudrama, in 'Storyteller'; fan fiction, in 'Superstar'), and consistently raises major ethical and ontological questions. Buffy herself, with her wit, strength and resource, is regularly held up as a new kind of female icon: in 2004 the Ofsted chief inspector David Bell suggested her as a role model for young girls failing the school system (apparently overlooking, as many commentators were quick to point out, the fact that she was expelled from her first school for burning it down).[31]

Buffy places Gothic squarely in the realm of teenagers: it maps the traumas of teenage existence back onto those of Gothic fiction so that high school literally is hell (or at least, on the mouth of it); the unsuitable older boyfriend is actually a vampire; and that awkward foreign exchange student a revivified Inca mummy. The centrality of adolescence to the programme's success is such that once Buffy and her friends reach their second university year, Buffy's younger sister Dawn is introduced, followed by an army of younger potential Slayers. Its relationship with Goth subculture, however, is more ambiguous, and it is this particular aspect of the show that I want to explore in more depth. Because of its positioning on the 'teenage Gothic' axis, Goths are one of the show's most significant, yet rarely acknowledged, audiences. As a series, *Buffy* both defensively pre-empts criticism that it is a 'Goth' show while simultaneously trading on Goth's appeal, exploiting Goth iconography in several of its most popular characters.

From informal evidence, Goths themselves appear to be ambivalent about *Buffy*. Some reject the show for its irreverence, or for its ostensibly populist immersion in the American high school genre. Others model themselves on characters like Spike, Angel and Drusilla, the show appearing to generate new interest in Goth among a younger generation. There is, of course, a range of responses between these two poles. I do not wish to speculate here on the opinions of an actual Goth audience for the show, although I do not doubt that one exists: clones of Spike, the black-clad, bleached-blond British vampire, can be found in small towns up and down the country. What interests me instead is how *Buffy* itself both acknowledges that audience and seeks to distance itself from it. As Justine Larbalestier has argued, *Buffy* periodically acknowledges its fans in self-reflexive episodes such as 'Superstar' and, subsequent to the publication of her article, 'Storyteller'.[32] *Buffy* does engage with Goth, but it does so with some hesitation, as if it is itself wary of being pigeon-holed as playing to a particular kind of audience. Incursions of Goth style into the narrative are rarely left unnoticed, but form the basis for self-reflexive comment and witty exchange.

'I'm a bloodsucking fiend, look at my outfit!': Vampirism and Performativity

In the Season Three episode 'Doppelgangland', Buffy's geeky best friend Willow, masquerading as her evil double, has recourse to her clothing in an attempt to 'prove' her evil credentials: 'I'm a bloodsucking fiend, look at my outfit!' Willow's exclamation is comic because the outfit does not convince us adequately that good Willow really is a bloodsucking fiend; the outward appearance is not enough to convey inner wickedness. Yet *Buffy* does consistently use clothing to convey evil. In 'The Wish', the first episode in which Evil Willow is introduced, the first signifier of difference between the 'real' Sunnydale and the Buffyless one wished into existence by Cordelia is the clothes. Ironically, in the alternative Sunnydale, it is the geeks, and not the fashion victims, who have the best outfits, as evidenced by Willow and Xander's S&M-inflected chic, in contrast to the drab costumes worn by 'popular' Harmony and her friends in their attempt to avoid attracting the vampires' attention. Not all vampires on *Buffy* inhabit the Goth vampire stereotype, but almost all of those who play major roles in the series engage with it on some level – the vampires Spike, Drusilla and Angel being the most significant. Furthermore, for all characters that embrace the livery of evil, there is a self-awareness and self-referentiality about what these clothes mean.

There are a number of episodes connecting Willow with performance and costume, often suggesting an anxiety about disjunction between internal and outward appearances. Although in itself a potentially interesting variation on Gothic conventions, this is of less interest here than what Willow's performance as her vampire alter-ego reveals about the performative nature of vampire identities. Good Willow in 'Doppelgangland' is forced to masquerade as her evil double, to put on the costume and perform the role of a vampire, a kind of 'vampire drag' analogous to the gender drag Judith Butler describes as revealing the performative nature of gender identities. For Butler, '*drag implicitly reveals the imitative structure of gender itself – as well as its contingency*'.[33] Vampire drag likewise reveals the imitative nature of vampire identity – that it too is an imitation without an original. In an alarmingly literal sense, one is not born a vampire, but becomes one. While the physical and spiritual state of being a vampire, like biological sex, is in most cases objectively determined (Angel and the neutered Spike are exceptions here), it is possible that vampire identity is, as Butler argues of gender, constituted from 'the stylized repetition of acts over time'.[34] These acts include fashion practices: dressing to be a vampire. Theoretically, a vampire in *Buffy* is recognizable as such only when its face changes. A vampire who does not attack should be undetectable to those without special Slayer knowledge. But those vampires who become consistent characters and therefore are frequently seen in non-vamp mode are usually still marked out as different, and dress is one distinctive aspect of this. Unlike the other inhabitants of Sunnydale, most of whom wear an approximation of what is currently fashionable, adapted to their particular character, the costumes of the major vampires have a timeless quality.

Indeed, the timelessness of their visual image might be a mark of the successful vampire: in a Season One episode, 'Welcome to the Hellmouth', Buffy identifies a soon-to-be-dusted vampire by dating his outfit to the 1980s. In contrast, Spike's, Angel's and Drusilla's costumes deliberately echo period styles, but are never historically accurate – not even in the flashback episodes. This in itself can be read parallel to the loose recycling of period styles common within Goth subculture.

Successful vampires, as opposed to those who appear briefly to be routinely disposed of, are suggestively dressed in a fashion appropriate to their role. Spike's and Drusilla's flamboyance in particular is a theatrical kind of wickedness, a relishing of the livery of evil. A regular writer and sometime co-producer, Marti Noxon, has stated that the inspiration for Spike and Dru were the Punk icons Sid and Nancy, but the proximity of Punk and Goth subcultures is clearly visible here, and this is a distinctly Gothicized Sid and Nancy, with a more self-consciously baroque element to the madness and mindless nihilism.[35] Subcultural rebels, they are irreverent of authority and tradition. Yet in their rebellion they conform to other vampire stereotypes: they look exactly as the vampire wannabes of the Season Two episode 'Lie to Me' might wish. Spike and Drusilla offer a kind of performance of vampireness, which in its very artificiality paradoxically makes them more effective. In Anne Rice's novel *Queen of the Damned* (1988), a newly woken ancient vampire finds he gets better results if he dresses up as Bela Lugosi. In a Baudrillardian move, the vampire as sign is more real than the authentic vampire. Spike and Drusilla present a distillation of the vampire self as performance. Giles's dream in 'Restless' shows Spike striking poses for assembled paparazzi: this vampiric voguing crystallizes Spike's performance into a few stylized gestures, explicitly recalling Butler's 'repeated stylization of the body'. Similarly, when Drusilla first becomes known to Buffy and her friends in 'Lie To Me', she is wearing a white empire-line dress. This style explicitly recalls the fashion prevalent at the turn of the eighteenth century, and typically clothed the heroines and anti-heroines of Gothic novels, but is anachronistic for Drusilla's own vampire life span – surely a self-conscious Gothicism. Vampires in quotation marks, Spike and Dru are nevertheless utterly convincing – with the possible exception of Juliet Landau's Cockney accent – but lots of vampires aren't: as Buffy tells Dracula at the beginning of Season Five, 'I've seen plenty of spotty, overweight vamps who call themselves Lestat'.

'Could you *have* a dorkier outfit?': Clothing and Subcultural Status

The problem of what constitutes an authentic vampire is one that is central to contemporary representations of the Goth community, as Katherine Ramsland's investigations, described above, show. While I would not wish to take Ramsland's account as necessarily representative of vampire-oriented subcultures in America, the competing claims to authentic subcultural identity she describes are a typical feature within studies of subcultures, and of Goth in particular. The playing off of vampire authenticity and fancy dress is directly addressed by *Buffy* in 'Lie To Me', in which Buffy saves a group of vampire worshippers from their delusions, demonstrating that vampires are not the romantic, 'exalted' figures they wish to believe. The vampire 'wannabes' are specifically portrayed as Goths, and as representatives of a type – 'I've seen this type before', Angel tells us. They inhabit an underground cellar decorated to look like a Goth nightclub, where Goth music is played and old vampire films are projected on the walls. Clothing too is that of the Goth underground, ranging from the attractive and reasonably convincing version of the look of the lead female wannabe, Chanterelle, to her male companion's ridiculous cape and ruffles, which provokes Buffy to exclaim: 'Could you *have* a dorkier outfit?' The wannabe's outfit is, indeed, dorky, a Hallowe'en costume rather than an accurate representation of subcultural style, but it is interesting that in this exchange Buffy reiterates the conventional playground division between those who affect fashionable, mainstream styles and 'alternative' types. Ramsland's efforts to 'pass' as a vampire are also resonant here in relation to Willow's and Xander's discomfort as they enter the wannabes' club: 'We blend right in. In no way do we stick out like sore thumbs', Willow remarks with bitter irony. The episode deliberately invokes a rhetoric of sartorial difference in which different levels of belonging and social status are multiply challenged and reinforced. In this playing off of sartorial distinctions, however, the Goths come off the worst: Goth is being presented here in a distinctly negative light. The programme places the viewers in an odd position. On the one hand, they are encouraged to view the wannabes as deluded and un-cool; on the other, the programme includes them (the viewers) amongst the privileged group of those 'in the know', those who are aware of the 'truth' about vampires. This might play in a straightforward, unproblematic fashion to a non-Goth audience. To Goth viewers, however, the effect is presumably more complex; if they are not to be alienated altogether, as indeed they might be, they must instead dismiss the wannabes as inferior or deficient Goths.

This manoeuvre is in fact integral to the functioning of subcultures. The pursuit of authenticity leads to the creation of hierarchies and rejection of those with less subcultural capital or commitment. Chanterelle and friends are clearly pretty committed to their subcultural identities, but, as their leader's Hallowe'en-style costume indicates, they are lacking in what Sarah Thornton, adapting Bourdieu, calls 'subcultural capital' – the insider knowledge that informs their subcultural status.[36] Yet at the same time, the 'authentic' vampires are also gently mocked for their lack of self-awareness. Angel insists that the vampire wannabes know nothing about how real vampires dress, only to be immediately confronted with a young man identically dressed to him. Of course, there is an upmarket but still distinctly Goth element to Angel's characteristic black attire. Thus the episode enables a double discourse, in which on the one hand Goth is disavowed,

Dark Willow does Goth power-dressing in Season Six of the TV show *Buffy the Vampire Slayer*, 2002.

presented as deluded and ludicrously costumed; on the other, Goth is recuperated through the glamour and charisma of its principal vampire characters.

'What's with the makeover of the damned?': The Recuperation of Goth Style

The process of recuperation, or smuggling of Goth back into *Buffy*, continues in the last three episodes of Season Six with the dramatic physical and sartorial transformation that Willow undergoes in her journey to the dark side. 'What's with the makeover of the damned?' is Xander's verbal quip in reaction to this transformation. As such, he deliberately references the common teen movie motif of the makeover, the sartorial transformation that signals the geek's initiation into the popular set, the rebellious teen's recuperation into polite mainstream culture. Examples are rife in teen films, from *The Breakfast Club* to *She's All That* (1999). The makeover as a fashion practice ultimately derives from nineteenth-century medical photography, when 'before' and 'after' photographs would be used to create a narrative of progress, in which the medically deficient subject would be manipulated or recuperated into a normalized social role. Teen makeovers, while lacking the medical pretext, perform much the same function: they offer the opportunity to make a 'better' self, implicitly a more normal self, feeding into a mainstream ethic of self-improvement, the fashion imperative becoming glossed with a moral one.

Willow's 'makeover of the damned' is the antithesis of the usual process of self-betterment: her change accentuates her difference, her lack of communality, her despair. If in the average teen movie the Goth is conventionally converted into the girl next door, then Willow's makeover operates in reverse, converting her bohemian chic of Season Six into what we might call Goth power-dressing. The progress narrative spirals into one of decadence and corruption; the peer-orchestrated transformation becomes inward and solipsistic; the magical transformation that is the desired outcome of the conventional makeover is literally enacted. Indeed, the distinction between evil and its successful performance that has been explored so playfully in *Buffy* for the previous five seasons is suddenly collapsed. Willow, who has displayed so much anxiety about performance and identity in previous episodes such as 'Nightmares' and 'Restless', is allowed to access a suggestively 'authentic' rage and supernatural force, in which power and difference are inscribed literally on and through her skin, hair and clothes. Having absorbed the text of the magic books through her skin, Willow no longer performs magic – she *is* magic.

To some extent, we might see the collapse of performativity in Dark Willow's suggestively Goth identity as a retrogressive movement, a deflation of the subversiveness and play found in the more performative Goth identities of Angelus, Spike, Drusilla and, indeed, the Evil Willow of Season Three. We might recall Giles's consoling fiction at the end of 'Lie To Me': 'the bad guys are always distinguished by their pointy horns or black hats'. In 'Villains' and the subsequent two episodes, *Buffy* comes as close as it ever does to confirming this fiction. As with Spike and Drusilla, Goth costume indicates a highly 'visible' evil: easily identifiable, reinscribing familiar iconography.

This is complicated, however, by the fact that Dark Willow undeniably looks extremely cool. Unlike the 'dorky' wannabes of 'Lie To Me', or Spike's 'skanky' Goth date in Season Six episode 'Hell's Bells', her look is invested with sex and power. This is 1990s designer Goth, rather than spectacular underground style. Willow's outfit recalls the *fin-de-siècle* high fashion purveyed by designers such as Alexander McQueen and Olivier Theyskens. While the 'Dark Willow' costume is obviously at some level a reprisal of the 'Evil Willow' of Season Three, it is less deeply embedded in the world of sexual fantasy or subcultural style, indexing instead a more serious, sophisticated, specifically adult power. Again, the programme flirts with Goth while subtly distancing itself from it, presenting a version of Goth filtered through the lens of upmarket fashion. In a twist on the conventional makeover motif, it is not the Goth who is recuperated, but Goth itself. Finally, *Buffy* manages to have its cake and eat it, exploiting the vivid sartorial vocabulary provided by Goth, while resisting the 'teenage Gothic' stereotype.

In *Buffy*, therefore, the contradictions between Gothic as mass entertainment and Goth as subcultural style are vividly evident. There is no easy resolution to this contradiction: the tension between the emptying out of meaning and the struggling for depth is the characteristic one of contemporary Gothic. There are differences, however, between specific modes of consuming the Gothic, and this is what the following chapter proposes to engage with.

A still from Tod Browning's *Dracula* (1931) showing Bela Lugosi in the title role.

CHAPTER FOUR

Gothic Shopping

Consuming Gothic

The history of Gothic has always been bound up with that of consumption, from the eighteenth-century association of the Gothic novel with luxury, a product with no intrinsic use value, to the court battle in 1963 between Bela Lugosi's family and Universal Studios over the rights to use the recently deceased *Dracula* star's image in lucrative merchandising. Crucially, Universal won, witnesses claiming that Lugosi was almost unrecognizable as Dracula, despite the fact that he wore almost no make-up for the role. The marketing image, not that of the actor himself, proved to be the 'authentic' one. As David J. Skal suggests in *Hollywood Gothic*, the trial itself was a kind of postmodern Gothic text: 'The image drains the actor in a Dracula / Dorian Gray / doppelganger fashion, he dies and is resurrected, his ghost employed to attract and fascinate children for purposes of economic exploitation. Vampirism and consumerism blur; one begets the other.'[1]

By the twenty-first century, however, the different means of marketing Gothic, or using Gothic to market other products, have become more varied, complex and nuanced than ever before. How, therefore, does one shop Gothically? Does one simply purchase Gothic objects, or is there a mode of consumption that is distinctly Gothic? This is not an easy question to answer. George Romero's classic horror film *Dawn of the Dead* (1979) depicted brain-dead zombies staggering vacantly through a shopping-mall to the sound of piped Muzak, the link between one form of mindless consumption and another comically underlined. Rob Latham has shown that our 'culture of consumption' can be mapped back onto Marx's description of capital as a vampire draining the life from the workers who labour to produce it. For Latham, 'youth consumption as a mode of cultural labor' replaces Marx's nineteenth-century factory workers.[2] In the twenty-first century, he suggests, 'consuming youth' becomes a dialectical image, as youth is both placed under a constant imperative to consume and in turn becomes an object of consumption, repeatedly offered up for our delectation through the imagery of film, television, fashion and advertising. According to Latham, the preoccupation with vampires and cyborgs within contemporary popular culture is an unconscious expression of Marx's logic:

> the vampire cyborg is such a potent figure that contemporary youth culture has virtually come to understand itself, albeit unconsciously, in its terms; popular vampire and cyborg texts effectively materialize the basic framework of Marx's dialectical critique of capitalist automation, now exported from the public site of the factory into the private domain of consumption and 'lifestyle'.[3]

As I suggested earlier, there are numerous similarities between the Gothic and the postmodern; Gothic adapts itself well to the conditions of late capitalism. I also cited E. J. Clery's argument that Enlightenment capitalism enabled the production of Gothic, in that only a culture that has ceased to entertain superstitious belief could turn superstition into a form of entertainment, ripe for mass consumption. What is more, according to Chris Baldick, Marx's description of the bourgeoisie also takes place in characteristically Gothic terms, as a haunted, *possessed* class, no more in control of its craving for surplus value than it is of the productive forces required to feed it ... The world-conquering bourgeoisie is seen in this new light as a thing driven by its addictions, a fugitive – like the Wandering Jew or Victor Frankenstein himself – in the grip of a more powerful demon of his own summoning.[4]

It seems as if the consumption-compulsion that drives the culture of late capitalism, where the bloodsucking factory owners of the nineteenth century have been replaced by the vampiric self-replication of the brand, may indicate that Western consumers are, as a group, possessed; that Gothic may offer a particularly suggestive mode for expressing the zeitgeist.

What this chapter sets out to do is look at the means through which Gothic and consumerism intersect through some specific examples. In the twenty-first century, the prevalence of Gothic-themed products make it easy to select Gothic as a lifestyle choice, with or without the commitment entailed by participating in Goth subculture. The rock star Cher has designed a range of Gothic furniture; Lawrence Llewelyn-Bowen offers Gothic as one of a series of BBC2 programmes on *Taste*, his own camp neo-dandyism a self-conscious imitation of Walpole and Wilde. The proud owners of the Gothic kitchen on *Taste* ('I saw it in the shop and I just had to have it') are mainstream, bourgeois, genteel – a far cry from the so-called Vampire Killers convicted in West Germany in 2002 or the Goths that mass at Whitby twice a year for the Whitby Gothic Weekend.[5]

The participants in Whitby Gothic Weekend, however, have their own forms of shopping. Paul Hodkinson's study of the provincial British Goth scene details a variety of strategies employed by subcultural consumers.[6] The most common objects of consumption are those that enable or enhance subcultural status, such as clothing, make-up, jewellery and music. The subjects of his survey buy most prominently from specialist shops, supplementing these purchases by ordering goods by mail order and

Contemporary Goth style
at Whitby Gothic Weekend,
April 2005.

Model Aimee Mullins in 'Access-
Able', from *Dazed and Confused*,
September 1998.

Trapped in a mirrored box: fashion itself as imprisoning agent of the Gothic in Alexander McQueen's show for London Fashion Week, 2001.

online, and, for some, finding items in mainstream shops and appropriating or customizing them. For Hodkinson, the integrity of Goth as a niche market, catered to mainly by producers already implicated in the subculture, has been instrumental to its coherence and longevity as a subcultural group.

I would argue, however, that the market for Gothic products is somewhat more complex than this, and involves both more overlap and finer distinctions between different kinds of consumers. For Ted Polhemus, writing in 1994, Goth is one of the few subcultures never to be appropriated by the mainstream, owing to its characteristic focus on the gloomy and morbid.[7] His statement, however, has perhaps proved somewhat premature, since the mainstream seems increasingly ready to consume Goth. In the late 1990s a number of high-profile designers, such as Alexander McQueen and Jean-Paul Gaultier, began to exploit Gothic images in their work. Some of these designs were inspired by Goth subculture, others – particularly those of McQueen and his collaborator, the jewellery designer Shaun Leane – appear to be inspired by a more intellectual consideration of Gothic discourses. Caroline Evans has written of how contemporary fashion design recycles fragments of the past in a way that invokes the return of the repressed, 'in which shards of history work their way to the surface in new formations and are put to work as contemporary emblems'.[8] She regards McQueen's work (both for his own label and for Givenchy) as a paradigmatic example of this process, and is particularly interested by McQueen's collection of spring / summer 1999, in which the amputee model Aimee Mullins showed off hand-carved prosthetic legs designed by McQueen, and the model Shalom Harlow 'revolved like a music box doll on a turntable as her white dress was sprayed acid green and black by two menacing industrial paint sprays which suddenly came to life on the catwalk'.[9] While not perhaps as overtly Gothic as some of McQueen's collections (inspired, for example, by Dante, Joan of Arc and the cult horror films *The Hunger* and *The Shining*), the kind of substitutions between human body and automaton that occurred in this show very specifically evoked the contemporary uncanny. As Evans indicates,

> Juxtaposing the organic with the inorganic (a model that mimicked a doll, a paint spray that mimicked human motions, and an artificial leg that enhanced human performance), the collection skewed the relation of object and subject to evoke Marx's nineteenth-century commodity exchange in which 'people and things traded semblances: social relations take on the character of object relations and commodities assume the active agency of people.' In the figures of these two young women the ghosts of Marx seemed to flutter up and live again at the end of the twentieth century, as the embodied forms of alienation, reification and commodity fetishism.[10]

The collection as a whole pointed to the constructed-ness of the human body: the moulded leather 'prosthetic' corsets designed by McQueen had breasts and nipples that suggestively replaced those of the wearer, yet were far from seamless constructions, bearing scars and stitches recalling Frankenstein's Creature. The body thus presented was artificial yet oddly organic, a protective shell that nevertheless bore the signs of injury, blatantly suggestive of the flesh even as it rendered it inaccessible to the touch. Above all, McQueen's corsets produced the body as surface, as fashioned from its garments, recalling the denial of depth Eve Sedgwick describes as the most characteristic feature of Gothic.[11]

McQueen's show of spring / summer 2001 was to take Gothic imagery to new extremes. The models paraded through a space contained within two-way mirrors, watched by the audience but able only to see themselves, thus neatly combining narcissistic doubling with voyeurism. At the end of the show, the sides of a glass box in the centre of the space fell open to reveal a naked, masked model smothered in moths, deliberately recalling the imagery of Joel-Peter Witkin. McQueen's imagery, like Witkin's,

Angelina Jolie in Versace at the 2000 Academy Awards ceremony.

evoked troubling, inarticulable desires. The audience was presented with the spectacle of fashion in decay: her dress having implicitly been eaten away, the model wore the living agents of its consumption. The opening of the box also suggested the moment of transformation when the adult insect emerges from the chrysalis – and the opening of Pandora's box, full of terrible secrets. If fashionable women are stereotypically compared to butterflies, then the moths seemed to imply a darker, more sinister face to the cliché, while the enclosing mirrors appeared to enact a motion whereby fashion itself became the imprisoning agent of the Gothic. McQueen presented fashion as a Gothic spectacle that seemed to gesture towards hidden meaning while self-reflexively pointing only to itself, reflecting back only perfect surfaces.

Work like McQueen's in turn influenced the high street, where it was possible to buy skull-and-crossbones bracelets from Top Shop, and deconstructed Victorian blouses from River Island. Individual Goth consumers may have chosen to signal their subcultural integrity by ignoring this mainstream trend, or may have enthusiastically embraced a rare instance of high-street stores catering to their taste. When dressed in the clothes, however, how could either strategy be told apart? This high street Gothicism is a rather different scenario from the mainstream incorporation of Punk shortly after its inception in the late 1970s. Punk style was arguably the invention of Malcolm McClaren and Vivienne Westwood anyway; and its adoption by the mainstream occurred within eighteen months or less of its formulation on the streets. In the quarter-century or so since Punk, the global exposure of new trends has accelerated to an unprecedented degree, due in no small part to the presence of the Internet as well as to trend scouts and image databases. New looks can now be displayed on the computer screens of designers all over the world within hours of their appearance on the street. In contrast, Goth had existed as a distinct entity for almost two decades before its appearance in the fashion world – a long time in the history of subcultures. Moreover, Goth is, itself, a look that recycles other looks – period costume, fetish wear, fancy dress (for example, fairy wings or cyborg goggles), even elements of Punk. The high-street appropriation of Goth style was therefore not only about the desire for the new, but also about a relationship with the old, with past looks – another kind of revival. Goth style did not provide the usual frisson of empty rebellion or packaged nostalgia provided by the appropriation or recycling of subcultural looks, but enabled a rather different set of sartorial meanings to be put into play.

It goes without saying that 1980s Goth superstars such as Siouxsie Sioux and their contemporary equivalents such as Marilyn Manson cultivate a highly public Goth style. Despite their critical and commercial success, they retain an identity invested with subcultural capital. When in 2000 the Hollywood actress Angelina Jolie wore jet-black hair extensions and a Gothic Versace gown to collect her Oscar for *Girl Interrupted*, however, the effect was entirely different. Jolie, at that time on the verge of A-list success, was also cementing a reputation as a rebel with a dangerous streak (she was known at that time for collecting knives, sporting multiple tattoos and writing her first husband's name on her wedding outfit in her own blood). She was instantly derided by the best-dressed lists for resembling Morticia Addams, and her outfit was sharply distinguished from the 'tasteful' black dress worn by her co-star (and sometime Goth pin-up) Winona Ryder for the same occasion. Jolie was able to present herself simultaneously as a bona fide member of the Hollywood A-list and as an edgy, rebellious outsider. Her tactical deployment of designer Gothic dress-up played on the darker side of her public image while still inserting herself within the discourses of mainstream celebrity. Despite subsequent highly publicized eccentricities, such as wearing a vial of her second husband's blood around her neck, Jolie nevertheless does not maintain the stylistic commitment to Goth distinctive of subcultural identity. Although her choice of a Gothic style on Oscar night was not empty consumption of the latest look – it was carefully selected to convey a particular identity and meaning – neither was it Gothic shopping in the subcultural mode.

In this chapter I want to look at two contrasting sites of Gothic consumerism in more depth. The first of these is the use of Gothic images in contemporary advertising; the second is the marketing of Gothic products that straddle the uneasy borderline between the subcultural and the mainstream. By focusing on these two particular examples, I hope to demonstrate something of the prevalence of Gothic in contemporary culture, and the ways in which it seems paradoxically both potent and redundant.

The Hideous Persuaders

In late 1999 an advertisement appeared in British cinemas promoting Smirnoff vodka. A young man of suggestively demonic aspect (possibly even the Prince of Darkness himself) appears striding purposefully through a ravaged urban environment. He is dressed in the late 1990s Goth style, strongly influenced by Marilyn Manson: long black hair, black leather trench coat, black cane. He enters a tattoo-removal surgery and shocks a grim-featured, sadistic nurse into submission by revealing a '666' tattoo on his scalp. The scene then cuts to a pastel-hued meadow in which the same young man, now dressed in a monk's habit with freshly shaved tonsure, is suggestively offered a cherry by an attractive young nun.

Smirnoff are well known for creative, edgy advertising campaigns that play with perceptions of fantasy and reality, such as their series of television and billboard campaigns in which everyday objects become startlingly exotic when viewed through the distorting lens of the Smirnoff bottle. Their pre-millennial cinema campaign, however, was surely more disturbing than waiters becoming penguins. This advertisement flirted quite openly with Satanism, body modification and Goth iconography. It was, in fact, the plot of Matthew Lewis's *The Monk* in reverse, set to an industrial / techno soundtrack. While the style and wit of the ad are compelling, it is hard to imagine the processes by which an advertising agency came to the conclusion that employing an overtly, even unsettlingly Gothic narrative and aesthetic was the best way to sell vodka. Why should a genre with distinctly unpleasant connotations (claustrophobia, fear, decay and moral turpitude) be revived as a means of selling alcohol?

The Smirnoff advertisement, however, is merely the most overt example of a minor but distinct trend that has developed over the last decade or so. Gothic imagery is most frequently employed in advertisements for alcoholic drinks – Tia Maria's 'Princess of Darkness' series and Metz's 'Judder Man' being the most memorable – but also in advertisements for washing powder, soft drinks, computer games, sunglasses, gas central heating and even Marmite. Who, exactly, is the target audience for these images? Arguably, they are part of a general trend towards ironic and morally ambiguous advertising, aimed at jaded postmodern audiences, the latest novelty in an industry that is always seeking the new. It is tempting, however, to seek a wider cultural significance within the appropriation of Gothic by the ultimate branch of consumerism.

The title of this section is a misappropriation of Vance Packard's infamous exposé of the American advertising industry, *The Hidden Persuaders*. Packard's book, first published in 1957, was a huge bestseller and is still in print today, at least partly because its sensational style contains more than a hint of a familiar Gothic conspiratorial plot. While there is not space to explore Packard's arguments in this book, it is worth drawing attention to the manner in which he expresses them. The eponymous Persuaders are sinister figures whose 'subterranean operations' consist of acquiring secret knowledge of the consumer – often figured as a housewife in a 'hypnoidal trance' – in order to manipulate their fears and desires, gaining control over their money and their minds.[12] Gothicized mechanisms of surveillance, the Persuaders recall J. Sheridan Le Fanu's villainous Uncle Silas, as George Orwell might have described him.

Since the publication of Packard's book, advertising has achieved a more ambiguous status in Western culture, becoming ever more pervasive even as its effectiveness is thrown into question. As Greg Myers suggests, ads are ubiquitous in Western culture but they are not omnipotent or monolithic.[13] Rather, he argues, they are made up of a number of different worlds that do not fit neatly together. The persuaders are no longer hidden but are rather increasingly clamouring for attention in a world in which they are as often analysed, critiqued or ignored by the consumer as they are absorbed. As such, advertisers have had to develop new methods of getting their message across. These are numerous, but include sponsorship, the ascendance of the brand over the product and self-reflexive advertising. Admen are no longer constructed as sinister figures; it is rather the ads themselves that may be sinister or shocking.

The use of Gothic images in advertising coincides with a broader trend away from traditional campaigns that associate their products with the satisfaction or pleasure to be gained by the consumer. An increasingly sophisticated, cynical and advertising-literate public is now wooed with a variety of tactics, including those referred to by Warren Berger as 'Shockvertising' and 'Oddvertising'.[14] 'Shockvertising' first appeared in the late 1980s, and deliberately aimed to stir up controversy through the use of violent, sexually explicit or politically contentious images. It deliberately flouted the 'positive register' in which most modern ads are framed, with the intention of polarizing its audience – and achieving further free exposure from the attendant press outrage. The brand most prominently associated with this strategy or set of strategies is Benetton, whose billboard campaigns representing AIDS victims and prisoners on Death Row were censured by left- and right-wing critics alike.

'Oddvertising', on the other hand, emerged in the late 1990s and is one of the most visible current trends. 'Oddverts' are weird, extreme and often inexplicable. Jettisoning the conventional logic of the advertisement, 'You will want to buy this because . . . ', they appeal instead to the irrational.

Paradoxically, however, this is a highly self-conscious and instantly recognizable form of the irrational: while Packard's hidden persuaders supposedly exploited subconscious desires, these adverts do so only in a stylized, self-conscious and irreverent way. In fact, these ads are often explicable through the categories of Surrealism and the Carnivalesque. Surrealism most often appears in ads for alcohol and cigarettes and, since the late 1980s, has become a relatively mainstream technique in advertising. It is a form of the irrational that permits a glossy surface and is contained in a recognizable cultural framework; it offers, therefore, a relatively 'safe' form of transgression perfectly commensurate with the dynamic of consumption.

The emergence of the Carnivalesque is more genuinely disruptive. The Tango advertisements of the 1990s can be placed in this category: the sudden appearance of a fat orange man who slaps Tango drinkers around the face suggests the kind of grotesque physical comedy and unruly laughter that Mikhail Bakhtin associates with Carnival. (Interestingly, this suggests that the appeal of 'Oddverts' is not entirely inexplicable after all.) While, of course, Tango ads are not Gothic by any stretch of the imagination, a Gothicized grotesque appeared in an advertisement for Marmite in 2002, in which an otherwise ordinary Marmite-eater was exhibited in a turn-of-the-century-style freak show. The 'I Hate Marmite' campaign as a whole intentionally exploited the somewhat irrational appeal of the tasty toast topping itself. By deliberately polarizing its audience into those who love and those who hate Marmite, the campaign successfully melded together the tactics of Oddvertising and Shockvertising. Indeed, in its self-conscious acknowledgement and encouragement of audience polarization, it could be labelled Post-Shockvertising.

Gothic ads often fall into one or both of these two categories. They frequently go against current advertising orthodoxy by employing a negative register, such as the evocation of Satanism in the Smirnoff advert described above. They also frequently employ the irrational or odd in an entirely self-conscious way. Metz's 'Judder Man' ads, for example, in which viewers were told to beware a jerkily animated, goblin-like figure, deliberately cultivated an aesthetic of the odd with precedents not only in Lewis Carroll's 'Jabberwocky' and the Struwwelpeter rhymes, but also in the Gothic animation of Tim Burton and, more specifically, Jan Svankmajer. There appeared to be no logical rationale to these adverts, but they were almost universally popular. In 2003 they were voted among the scariest screen moments ever by the viewers of Channel 4.[15]

At this point it is important to qualify the use of the word Gothic in relation to advertising images. I am not necessarily arguing for the status of the majority or even necessarily any of these advertisements as Gothic in themselves. What I am suggesting, however, is that certain contemporary advertisements plunder images associated with a Gothic aesthetic, from stock characters such as Dracula and Frankenstein's monster to sinister or macabre plotlines or visual references. Relocated into a new context, these images often become 'de-Gothicized', stripped of their connotations of terror, the macabre or the sublime and made cosy and wholesome. Nevertheless, they remain in dialogue with the genre from which they originate, and contribute to the contemporary understanding of Gothic in the public consciousness.

The most common means of employing Gothic imagery in advertising is to capitalize on its familiarity. Often exploiting the iconic images of the Lugosi Dracula or the Karloff Frankenstein, these adverts usually parody Gothic narrative or invert its conventions to comic effect. Hence an ad of 2002 for the Orange mobile network, which showed a cartoon vampire strolling around in broad daylight in order to publicize its cheap daytime calls. Consumers don't expect cheap calls during the day; nor do they expect Dracula in the daylight. Ads of this type form a kind of anti-Gothic, which conforms to the more traditional advertising strategy of suggesting the product can improve your life. By using his Orange phone Dracula is no longer doomed to imprisonment in the same morbid cycle of convention. He has been freed from generic constraints. This comic deflation of Gothic is in fact reassuring rather than disturbing. Dracula's recognition value makes him a cosy rather than threatening figure. Dracula himself is perhaps a kind of brand – and as all good advertising executives know, consumers like brands they can recognize. The very repetitiveness of Gothic, which is one of its distinguishing characteristics, one of its potentially most disturbing effects and one of its main pleasures, here functions to undo itself – and of course to sell mobile phones. A number of recent advertisements have used similar storylines. One for Mini cars showed a swarm of zombies getting bored and going home because the Mini containing a courting couple proved impenetrable; another particularly inventive ad showed a fitter installing British Gas at the suburban home of Satan, with Cerberus lounging by the gas fire.

For Fred Botting, such use of stock Gothic characters signals their transformation into myth, in the sense defined by Roland Barthes in *Mythologies* (1973). For Barthes, something becomes a myth when it becomes detached from the social, historical and political context in which it was formed, becoming a universally recognizable idea or image. Ideologically, myth embarks on a project of simplification or purification, reducing complex issues to the status of the natural and eternal. Discussing the electricity privatization adverts that appeared on British TV in the early 1990s and which featured a comic Frankenstein figure, Botting writes:

> *Frankenstein*, much discussed and greatly reworked, has been thoroughly transformed and purged of any threatening significance . . .
> *The Munsters*, *The Addams Family* and even *The Flintstones* have turned the disturbing Karloffian monster into a genial, ineffectual and laughable figure. Taming the monster, the threatening Other is incorporated within safe and recognisable limits.[16]

For Botting, nevertheless, the ad campaign employed the *Frankenstein* myth for the purpose of putting across a very specific political agenda, one that uses laughter in order to represent an old mythology of the state and labour as 'redundant . . . an unnatural monster' and reorient its audience to a new mythology of privatization.[17] In this instance, the utilization of Gothic archetype was complex and politically charged, but this is not generally the case in Gothic advertising. The Orange mobile phone ad might distantly recall the embrace of contemporary technologies in Bram Stoker's *Dracula*, suggesting that this vampire revenant is able to survive by his embrace of the modern world, but the link is tenuous and unlikely to be grasped by the majority of viewers.

If such ads deploy the recognition value of Gothic 'myths' such as Dracula and Frankenstein or typical Gothic narrative conventions within a comic register, others take the opposite tactic and exploit the qualities of mystery, danger and the unexpected that Gothic images afford. These advertisements combine the irrational appeal of 'Oddvertising' with the suggestively sexual lure of the fantastic and supernatural. Tia Maria's 'Princess of Darkness' ad from 1999, for example, showed its eponymous heroine using mysterious forces to draw a hunky young film actor to her lair in order to open a pickle jar. Notwithstanding the bathos of this outcome, and the phallic connotations of the gherkin, this remains a confusing and inexplicable ad, one that appears to gesture towards a hidden meaning that perhaps does not exist. As such it suggestively presents the Princess of Darkness as a kind of hidden (rather than hideous) persuader in herself. However, there is also a much more conventional element in the Tia Maria advertisements, which simply presents Gothic as mysteriously sexy – a kind of Scottish Widows effect. A typical 1990s woman, the Princess of Darkness gets what she wants and is in control, even if she can't manage (or can't be bothered) to open her own pickles. Although the brand's slogan is, 'Have *you* met the Princess of Darkness?', it appears that the ad is targeted not at men wanting to meet her but at women wanting to be like her. (Women are purportedly the primary consumers of liqueurs.) A preceding advertisement in the series, in which a man disappears without explanation without his clothes after meeting the Princess of Darkness in a bar, similarly elides mystery, danger and sex. It directly prefigures the Impulse 'Siren' campaign of 2003, in which the camera pans across a series of 'missing' posters pinned to trees while a haunting, bluesy refrain asks 'Where have all the young men gone?' After a lone young man disappears from his seat in a café, we see him meet a young woman beside a river. The overt message is clearly that he has been drawn there by her perfume, which is irresistible to men, but since the subtext appears to be that she is either supernatural or some kind of serial killer (or possibly both), the appeal is somewhat darker than most perfume advertisements, the opening shots of the endlessly repeated 'missing' posters providing the genuine chill of the uncanny.

The Smirnoff advert depicting the adventures of Damien is a kind of masculine version of the Tia Maria and Impulse ads. It clearly played on the millennial preoccupations of the period in which it was released, the '666' tattoo suggesting 'the number of the beast' from the biblical book of Revelation. At first glance, it is a daring and transgressive advert, playing for a sophisticated audience. It operates according to a set of fixed binary oppositions: good and evil, sacred and profane, innocence and experience, pastoral and urban. These are disrupted by the central figure, whose manipulation of surface symbols enables him to traverse the two opposed worlds constructed by the ad. The tag-line, 'Pure Smirnoff', is thus subverted in order to suggest that although the vodka may possess the semblance of purity, it is actually attractively wicked – a variation on the 'naughty but nice' or 'devilishly good' theme. 'Pure' maintains the associations of 'clear', 'absolute', 'genuine' and so on, but is divested of less attractive moralistic connotations.

The advertisement also demonstrates a striking literacy in the Gothic themes of disguise and its relation to the self. Here, Smirnoff suggestively enables authentic identity to be disguised: with the erasure of the identifying mark (666 on the scalp), the wicked self, which is the protagonist's 'true' identity, is hidden beneath a mask of purity. Damien becomes a 'white devil': his new, duplicitous identity remains available to the viewer but not to the saintly objects of his lust. If, as Eve Sedgwick has argued, the Gothic convention of writing on flesh amounts to a form of repetition, re-iterating the identity of that which it marks, the '666' advertisement suggests that modern laser technology has the ability to reverse this process, reducing the satanic symbol to the status of mere fashion mistake. On one level it supports an essentialist notion of identity – Damien is just as wicked dressed as a monk as he is in Goth garb – on another, signs of identity become fluid and manipulable, to the extent that a symbol as irrevocable as the mark of the beast can be reversed.

Despite its Gothic trappings, nevertheless, the advertisement conforms to the 'New Lad' ethos of the late 1990s: the Prince of Darkness acquires his disguise not in order to destroy the world, create chaos and mayhem, or even (primarily) to corrupt souls – rather, simply in order to have more sex. Evil is presented as sexy and pleasurable to a modern audience – not really evil at all in fact, just a little bit naughty. Despite an element of camp, furthermore, which is provided by the 'Pierre et Gilles' style soft focus of the pastoral landscape and the kitsch titillation, any naughtiness about to take place is presented as definitively heterosexual, its transgressive quali-ties deriving merely from the compromising of chastity, no longer a highly prized virtue in contemporary British culture. As such the advertisement performs a not dissimilar role to the ostensibly much 'safer' ad for Archers featuring the popular TV actor James Lance as a 'lad' who sneaks home late and sleeps on the sofa so as not to disturb his girlfriend, only for the viewer to see her tiptoeing past him up the stairs even later still. Both advertise-ments are purveying the same message – drink Archers / Smirnoff and get up to more stuff that perhaps really you shouldn't (without getting found out); each simply seeks to establish through atmosphere and aesthetic a distinctive identity for their product. This is the reason, perhaps, why Gothic works particularly well in drinks advertising – people don't generally drink in order to be 'good' or improve their lives. Transgressive behaviour fits with the desired outcome of using the product.

Despite the edgy visuals, thundering soundtrack and demonic overtones, therefore, the Smirnoff advertisement offers a very 'safe' transgression: one that flirts with Satanism in order to lend a dangerous edge to its product but nullifies offence by retreating into a heterosexualized camp. Cleverly, furthermore, it manages to have it both ways in terms of target audience: leaving the subcultural image it deploys intact (sustaining the associations of Goth with sexiness, danger and transgression), while exploiting its spectacular qualities for a mainstream audience. It is, paradoxically, a deliberately offensive advertisement that simultaneously avoids offending as many people as possible. Ultimately, it provides little more genuinely to disturb than does the Orange cartoon vampire.

Advertising is an inherently parasitic form, one that indiscriminately vampirizes popular culture for its own ends, often draining the life from the thing it vampirizes in the process. As such there is no coherent, identifiable way that ads use anything, much less a set of discourses as diverse as Gothic. The influx of Gothic imagery into advertising in the late 1990s passively reflects a contemporary trend in music, fashion and film as much as it actively proposes an agenda of its own. While individual ads may use Gothic to make individual statements about their products, or to differentiate them from other similar products, ultimately this says more about the process of creating brand distinction than it does about targeting a particular market. It seems unlikely that the size of the market addressed by a brand like Smirnoff (or Tia Maria, or Orange) could be much enhanced merely by the members of a niche subcultural audience. Rather, the familiarity of Gothic imagery to a mainstream audience makes it easy to plunder, while its visually striking or thematically extreme nature makes it distinctive and memorable – all, of course, desirable qualities within advertising.

The Pursuit of the Undead Dollar

There are products, however, that are directly marketed to that niche audience, and it is to these that I now turn. In 1987 the Goth band The Sisters of Mercy went into the Top 10 with a single called *This Corrosion*. Produced by Jim Steinman, better known for his work with Meatloaf, the song commercialized the Sisters' trademark sepulchral vocals and deep basslines by marrying them with clarity of sound, soaring church choirs and an anthemic chorus complete with high-energy female backing vocals.

Quite apart from the irony of this group's conversion of the doom-laden Goth sound into chart fodder, the song itself seems to indicate an awareness of the deliberate marketing of otherness, of subcultural difference, to a mainstream audience. One of the singer Andrew Eldritch's lyrics invokes 'Selling the don't belong': a more subtle means, perhaps, of defining selling out – less compromising your ideals for money than embracing corrosion or decadence by selling the identity of the outsider.[18] Eldritch here seemed to anticipate a major theme of Goth subculture in the 1990s and beyond: that in order to survive, it has had to find ways of negotiating an increasingly consumerized counter-culture.

The argument that subculture is fundamentally opposed or resistant to a mainstream consumer culture is a naïve one, and has been repeatedly contested by subcultural theorists. Angela McRobbie, for example, has argued for recognition of the economic activities that support subcultures (such as selling second-hand clothing).[19] This argument is taken up by Paul Hodkinson's *Goth*: for Hodkinson, Goth subculture is imbued in economic transactions – the selling of records, clothing, make-up and jewellery, for example. It is still, nevertheless, remarkably distinct from the mainstream market. The marketing of products to Goths in fact often uses a perceived non-mainstream identity as a selling point, emphasizing the difference prized by members of the subculture.

Nevertheless, in the last few years there has been a surge of products associated with a Gothic aesthetic that have outgrown or surpassed conventional subcultural markets. One of the most prominent of these is Emily the Strange, a women's skate-wear label that features T-shirts and other items of clothing emblazoned with wittily macabre designs, all featuring the cartoon figure of Emily herself or her black cat familiars. Emily the Strange has been so successful that it has branched out into a range of accessories including toys, lunchboxes, perfume and even bath-mats and shower curtains. Emily the Strange has featured in fashion publications as diverse as *The Face*, *Elle* and the style pages of *The Guardian*, and is reportedly worn by the grunge rock star turned Hollywood icon Courtney Love. Similar clothing labels, such 'Ruby Gloom', featuring a scarlet-haired Goth girl, 'Roman Dirge', and 'Mary Mary', all similarly featuring cartoon Goth characters, have been swift to cash in on the trend.

As already noted, Goth subculture is dependent on the manufacture and sale of products that enable its musical and sartorial stylings. To a certain extent, Emily the Strange and Ruby Gloom fit into this pre-existing pattern of subcultural consumption. Available only from specialist cloth-ing shops or from Internet shopping sites, Emily the Strange and Ruby Gloom demand a certain degree of insider knowledge, even if that exclu-sivity is increasingly eroded by mainstream media coverage. Moreover, the product sold is predominantly clothing, which is, along with music, a cornerstone of the subcultural marketplace. Style and musical taste have always been regarded as two of the crucial markers of subcultural affiliation, and these needs have traditionally been met by both mainstream and subcultural producers.

More interesting is the development of 'Gothic' themed products that do not fulfil these traditional subcultural needs. Prominent among these are the Living Dead Dolls, a range of macabre adult toys including a disfigured prom queen, a straitjacketed lunatic and a manic clown, all presented in their very own cardboard coffins. The creators, Ed Long and

Living Dead Dolls exclusive set, 'Nosferatu and Victim', released 2003.

Damien Glonek, began by making hand-made dolls to sell at toy fairs, before signing up with the American toy company Mezco in 2000 and releasing, to date, nine main series of dolls plus four series of mini-dolls and a variety of spin-offs and special limited editions, including a European-only Jack the Ripper doll and an American-only Girl Scout – appropriately named Cookie. While the dolls have been phenomenally successful – each series having a bigger production run than the last – they have retained cult credibility through limited distribution, hard-to-find 'exclusives' and the cultivation of an aura of maverick creativity by Long and Glonek, who regularly appear at toy fairs and comics conventions to greet their fans. The brand has recently spawned several second-rate imitators, indicating the strength of the market.

Living Dead Dolls, while clearly designed with Gothic themes and presumably Goth consumers in mind, do not enable the cultivation of subcultural style or musical knowledge in the individual. Neither do they directly enable the forging of subcultural communities through social events. While many fans of the dolls may deliberately seek out other fans on the Internet or at toy fairs, this is secondary to the purpose of purchasing and collecting the dolls and is by no means participated in by all collectors.

Furthermore, the degree of financial investment required by Living Dead Dolls collectors is phenomenal, challenging that of the most serious record collectors. A new doll retails (at the time of going to press) for around £20, making the cost of each series at least £100 altogether. However, many fans began collecting relatively late into the dolls' development, creating intense demand for the first three series of dolls in particular. The rarest and most popular dolls now reach dramatically inflated prices on Internet auction sites. It is common for toy collectors to buy two copies of an item, one to keep pristine and one to play with; but collectors of Living Dead Dolls frequently also buy a copy to customize. While Long and Glonek claim that they design the dolls for love not money, and that they still have to hold down day-jobs, the burgeoning range of spin-off products, including clothing, stationery, a board game and fairy lights, puts their discourse of subcultural authenticity in conflict with one of opportunist capitalism. This apparent contradiction is one that many of the more-than-1,000 fans using the official message board have chosen to comment on.

These practices are less congruent with the traditional ones of Goth subculture, which include dressing up, listening to music and attending Goth events, and more allied to those of 'fan' culture. Fan culture is usually based around cult films, TV programmes or comics and frequently involves the purchase of themed collectibles. While Living Dead Dolls can be bought in some specialist clothing shops, particularly the American chain Hot Topic, and, more recently, music shops like HMV and Tower

Records, they are more commonly found in comic shops or online sites dedicated to cult toys and collectibles. For example, in the mail-order catalogue for Forbidden Planet, a prominent company catering to these consumers in the UK, Living Dead Dolls feature alongside merchandise for *Buffy the Vampire Slayer, Lord of the Rings, Star Wars* and *The Simpsons*. The Dolls are in the minority of products in the catalogue that are not explicitly tied in to a film or television franchise. Significantly, the first, hand-made dolls were produced by Long and Glonek in 1998, one year after the series *Buffy the Vampire Slayer* first aired on American TV. While this should be seen in terms of Zeitgeist rather than influence, Long and Glonek certainly benefited from the kind of market the programme created. After *Buffy* (itself heavily merchandised), the witty repackaging of Gothic themes for a teen / twenty-something audience became a profitable business strategy.

Cult collectibles characteristically fulfil a particular purpose: to enable the fan to extend their involvement with their chosen film or show beyond the initial experience of watching it. The most successful examples of film and TV merchandising ultimately are able to stand alone from the experience of viewing; for example, the Superman logo or Disney's Mickey Mouse character. This is not the case with the majority of what I am calling cult collectibles, most of which are meaningless without prior specialized knowledge of the film or TV programme concerned. The display of such items is in fact a means of making visible that specialist knowledge, signifying one's membership of a fan community. This is particularly important for those fan cultures that do not have a means of signifying group belonging through dress – unlike spectacular subcultures such as Goths, fans tend to be lacking in a distinctive, unifying style. Thus the predominantly (though not exclusively) male consumers of cult collectibles convert their initial experience of media consumption into a statement of lifestyle.

Interestingly, Living Dead Dolls seem to tap into a female demographic not otherwise exploited by the cult collectibles market. Dolls are characteristically feminized objects, where models of monsters and aliens are not. While Living Dead Dolls are frequently despised or ignored by collectors of conventional dolls such as porcelain figures or Barbies, their combination of cult appeal with a traditionally feminized object enables them to appeal to young women as well as men (although it should be stressed that there are also many male collectors of Living Dead Dolls). The dolls themselves are roughly 80 per cent female, and the most popular dolls in each series have so far always been female. No doubt this is partially because of culturally prescribed associations between dolls and femininity – or perhaps the fact that the female dolls simply have better clothes.

As has been amply shown by Henry Jenkins in his book *Textual Poachers*, fans are not merely passive consumers but are able to fashion new cultures and communities from the scraps and fragments they scavenge from the media, a process he terms 'textual poaching'.[20] Living Dead Dolls are particularly interesting within the fan market in that they seem to elicit very specific kinds of fan 'poaching' practices. Collectors literally refashion their dolls by customizing them, creating new characters or new looks for original characters. Recent custom dolls displayed on the fan message board include dolls made to look like horror-film characters such as Beetlejuice and Carrie, and original characters such as – my particular favourite – Anakalia, 'a drowned surfer who hit her head on the sharp rocks below'.[21] Many dolls are also customized to look more like Goths or given additional tattoos and piercings, echoing the subcultural style's self-customizations. Indeed, the range of characters embodied by the Living Dead Dolls tends to reflect those appropriated by Goth style, suggesting that even when the dolls are not directly consumed by Goths themselves, they replicate Goth identities. Fans also create photo-narratives featuring the dolls, ironically replaying the conventional boy-meets-girl photo-stories of teenage magazines. These narratives, however, are usually given a blackly humorous twist, often involving imaginative use of accessories as murder weapons. Thus the collection of Living Dead Dolls need not be seen as an anomaly in Goth subcultural practice, if Goth is itself understood as a hybrid of spectacular and fan subcultures, a culture that has always been dependent not only on dramatic sartorial style but also on the 'poaching' or rewriting of other narratives, those of Gothic literature and film. Each of the Dolls is itself a mini-narrative, both the culmination of a variety of Gothic traditions and the starting point from which fans can create new narratives of their own.

In Hélène Cixous's rereading of E.T.A. Hoffmann's 'The Sandman', she argues that if, in Freud's famous reading of the tale, the uncanny is the fear of castration, the female equivalent is the fear of being turned into a doll, like Hoffmann's Olympia.[22] If for Cixous the uncanny doll represents the fear of being objectified, of being made into an 'other', then fans' use of Living Dead Dolls would appear to offer a particularly interesting response to this reading. Living Dead Dolls are self-consciously sinister; their uncanniness is predetermined. As such they seem to be perversely comforting to their fans, a means of rejecting conventional stereotypes of 'good' femininity associated with traditional dolls. Many of the dolls are travesties of conventional stereotypes of 'good' women, from a nurse and a nun to a cheerleader and even an Easter bunny. Others are rebellious archetypes such as Lilith or historically deviant women such as Lizzie Borden. Moreover, the fans' customization and dramatization of their dolls suggest a way in which they are able to resist objectification, piecing together their own narratives and set of icons. The fact that many of these dolls, both official releases and customs, are based on pre-existing images of femininity should not be seen as diminishing the power and pleasure they afford their fans. The sense of play and fantasy self-creation that is enabled by the dolls resists superficial stereotype.

The associations of the dolls with childhood are also particularly contentious. When the Hollywood-themed Series Five was released, many fans commented unfavourably that the dolls looked too 'adult', and that they preferred the earlier, more childlike designs. This debate was repeated with even greater vehemence on the release of the 'Fashion Victims', a line that refigured some of the most popular dolls as zombie fashion models. Arguably, part of the dolls' appeal is that they represent not only 'bad' women but also 'bad' children: children who are playful, rebellious, naughty, do not conform. A creator of custom dolls who makes over the Living Dead Dolls to look conventionally 'cute' – pre-dead dolls, if you like – regularly causes heated controversy on the website's message board. For some fans, removing the self-consciously disturbing aspect of the dolls paradoxically seems to make them more disturbing, turning them into emblems of conformity and sentimental attitudes to childhood. If contemporary American culture has a fixation with childhood trauma narratives – adult problems as a consequence of repressed traumatic memory – then the Living Dead Dolls can be seen as enacting a form of resistance to those narratives. The dolls present a version of childhood that is playful but not innocent. Each of the dolls has suggestively undergone a trauma – they are accompanied by a piece of doggerel verse in which the circumstances of their death are revealed – yet this is presented as a source of pleasurably macabre narrative, albeit one that the doll is nominally doomed to repeat. The fans who create new narratives around their dolls suggestively release them from this predetermined role – a message-board debate following the issue of boy doll Tragedy, for instance, who allegedly could not bear to be separated from his lost (female) love Misery, has humorously enquired whether he is actually gay.

Ed Long and Damien Glonek have insisted in interviews that the dolls are just that, dolls, and not representations of dead children. They have, apparently, only ever received one letter of complaint; most consumers, it would seem, are quite capable of viewing the dolls as fantasy. The dolls themselves are all marked 'Age 15 and Up', signalling their intended adult audience, although anecdotal evidence would suggest that younger children are fascinated by them too. Nevertheless, Long's and Glonek's comments appear somewhat disingenuous. It is difficult to avoid the perception that it is precisely the conjunction between innocence and experience, the cute and the horrid, that makes the dolls so exciting to their collectors. As their oxymoronic name suggests, the dolls are inherently paradoxical, living and dead, inhabiting a series of borderlines in paradigmatically Gothic fashion. Their contradictory natures enable their collectors symbolically to resolve the contradictoriness of their own position, as rebellious consumers, who wish to signal their difference from conventional lifestyle choices at the same time as they participate in the process of consumption. The dolls permit their owners to purchase Gothic as a lifestyle, to 'own Goth', yet simultaneously to engage in a series of expressive practices through which they can assert individualized identities. To return to the quotation from The Sisters of Mercy given earlier in this section, 'Selling the don't belong': not to belong is also not to be at home – in other words, *unheimlich*. By buying these uncanny dolls, Goth consumers can also make themselves feel *heimlich*, at home, creating a sense of comfort and stability around their own identity choices.

The Living Dead Dolls represent a new kind of Gothic shopping. They can be bought throughout America, Western Europe and Japan, and yet retain an aura of cult credibility. They signal both underground commitment and the joys of the global marketplace. As such they embody a new Gothic: Gothic as pure commodity, pure luxury, pure excess. This new Gothic possesses the same properties as its eighteenth-century precedents but more so: no longer anchored to the page or the screen, Gothic fantasy floats free in the marketplace.

Conclusion:
The End of Gothic?

'The road of excess leads to the palace of wisdom.'

William Blake, *The Marriage of Heaven and Hell* [1]

If Gothic discourses have reached an unprecedented level of ubiquity in contemporary culture, then for some critics this signals imminent exhaustion. Fred Botting in particular has delineated the gaping void that exists at the core of contemporary Gothic, coining the term 'Candygothic' to refer to a mode of horror figured as consumption, as a lavish sweetshop of horrid thrills that ultimately fail to satisfy:

> 'Candygothic' signifies an attempt to reassess the function of horror in a (western) culture in which transgressions, taboos, prohibitions no longer mark an absolute limit in unbearable excess and thus no longer contain the intensity of a desire for something that satisfyingly disturbs and defines social and moral boundaries. Though numerous figures of horror are thrown up by contemporary fiction and film – Krugers, Chuckies, Pinheads,

Lecters, their shelf-life seems limited in the face of a demand for more thrilling horrors, their terror index-linked to the novelties provided by special effects, visual techniques and stylised killing.[2]

Elsewhere, Botting notes that 'Gothic fiction, which served as earlier modernity's black hole and has served up a range of objects and figures crystallising anxiety into fear, has become too familiar after two centuries of repetitive mutation and seems incapable of shocking anew.'[3] Gothic may be a set of discourses that thrives on revival, but in the context of post-modernity this process has been short-circuited, the production of meaningful terror stymied by the channelling of excess through the path of least resistance. Where once Gothic provided a space in which the dark dreams of the Enlightenment could be realized, now it simply exposes the void at the heart of an advanced consumer culture: 'Once the dark under-side of modernity, Gothic horror now outlines the darkness of the postmodern condition.'[4]

Botting's analysis is trenchant, but perhaps overly pessimistic. For all its thrills and chills, Gothic has always, ultimately, been rather reliable, and not just in a generic sense. Certainly, we can rely on Gothic to provide pleasurable suspense, luxurious terror and wicked humour. This is simply generic expectation. However, there is also a sense in which Gothic can be relied on to fulfil whatever cultural or critical need arises at any given time. In the early days of academic criticism, Gothic was often defined through a list of stock elements, such as crumbling castles, supernatural visitations and persecuted heroines. Many recent critics, some of whom I have discussed, have attempted to provide a more succinct, cohesive explanation of Gothic, an explanation that does not have to resort to this schematic 'shopping list' of components. Perhaps Gothic is, as they have argued, about the return of the repressed, or the combined pressures of returning history and constrictive geography, or the privileging of surface over depth, or anachronistic survivals of the past into the present. Or perhaps it is so amenable to these theories, and indeed to contemporary interpretations in general, because its components can be reordered in infinite combinations, because they provide a lexicon that can be plundered for a hundred different purposes, a crypt of body parts that can be stitched together in myriad different permutations. Ultimately, perhaps, the resurgence of Gothic in so many different areas of contemporary culture arises from different, localized needs rather than one over-arching one. It can be progressive or conservative, nostalgic or modern, comic or tragic, political or apolitical, feminine or masculine, erudite or trashy, transcendently spiritual or doggedly material, sinister or silly. It is difficult to say what contemporary Gothic 'is', or even what it is like, since it does all these things so well. The label 'Gothic' is convenient because it can be applied to so many artefacts, but it could be argued that Gothic itself is convenient. It is itself a perfect product, readily available and simply adapted to the needs and purposes of a wide variety of consumers. The ultimate luxury, as Clery described its eighteenth-century precedents, contemporary Gothic seldom fails to be entertaining. It quickens the pulse and heightens the senses. It appeals to the contemporary lust for spectacle and sensation. This does not prevent it, however, from offering genuine and incisive comment on the world. It is true that Gothic, in its most recent incarnation, has become the stuff of lifestyle, one consumer choice among many. But individual consumption is not without its politics: individual consumer choices can indicate renegotiations of identity politics at a micro-level. The Living Dead Dolls phenomenon, for example, suggests something very interesting about the constructions that particular groups of consumers place on contemporary childhood. The ascendance of Gothic comedy, likewise, need not be seen as a vacating of significance, but rather as eliciting a new set of meanings that may be harder to identify, but which deliver meaning nevertheless. Moreover, there is ample evidence that politics at a macro level are more significant within Gothic fictions than ever before. Seen as a mode in which one of the dominant features is the repercussion of the past within the present, Gothic offers a unique and flexible tool for various kinds of political comment, enabled by that very self-consciousness facilitated by the conditions of postmodernity. Toni Morrison's *Beloved* (1987) is the most prominent example of how this could function, in its story of a community of nineteenth-century black Americans haunted by the traumas of slavery. Beloved, the strange young woman who seems to be the phantom embodiment of a murdered child, is the catalyst through which the historical horrors of slavery are exposed and not quite exorcised. Beloved reminds the characters of events in their past of which they do not want to be reminded, but need to address in order to move on. As such it offers a kind of monument to the dead, a testament rather than a tombstone. As Chris Baldick suggests, 'we can conclude that while the existential fears of Gothic may concern our inability to escape our dying bodies, its historical fears derive from our inability finally to convince ourselves that we have really escaped from the tyrannies of the past. The price of liberty, as the old saying tells us, is eternal vigilance.'[5]

Gothic has always had a political dimension: in the eighteenth century, it was profoundly implicated in the discourses of revolution. Edmund Burke's use of a Gothic idiom to describe the French revolutionaries' attack on Marie Antoinette in his *Reflections on the Revolution in France* (1790) indicates that Gothic terrors and political terrors have been imbricated over a long history.[6] Ronald Paulson, in *Representations of Revolution*, traces at length the way that contemporary events became figured in eighteenth- and nineteenth-century Gothic novels.[7] In Lewis's *The Monk*, for instance, the scene in which a murderous mob set fire to the abbey strongly recalls the storming of the Bastille. On a more complex level, Paulson demonstrates how the progress of the protagonist – from a state of repression, to the throwing off of repression, to becoming worse than his original oppressors – reflects the progress of the Revolution itself. Yet, as he explains, there is no clear political message provided by the novel, revolutionary events apparently plundered largely for sensational effect.

I have already suggested, in my discussion of the *Aztecs* exhibition in the Introduction, the kinds of cultural work Gothic discourses may perform in relation to prevailing ideologies, even in contexts apparently quite dislocated from an obvious Gothic tradition. I have also suggested, following the Marquis de Sade, that in times of terror authors might 'turn to hell for aid' in order to titillate a jaded populace. It would be equally possible to argue that at times of genuine terror Gothic becomes redundant – noting, for example, the apparent loss of interest in Gothic writing in Europe during the two World Wars. This book was first conceived shortly after 9/11, and in those early months it did seem as if the fall of the Twin Towers might mean the end of Gothic – or at least the phase of it that was in full swing at the turn of the millennium. A few years into the new century, however, it appears that our appetite for Gothic continues unabated, and the form has simply shifted to encompass the time's sensibilities. Johan Höglund has suggested that the development of American imperialism has led to a revivification of the motifs of late nineteenth-century imperial Gothic in contemporary Hollywood: the film *Van Helsing* (2004), for example, remodelling Dracula in the image of Osama bin Laden.[8] Gothic perhaps also retains what Chris Baldick has referred to as a 'homeopathic' function.[9] The astonishing success of Dan Brown's pot-boiler, *The Da Vinci Code* (2003), in which religious conspiracy and occult secrets are uncovered through the study of ancient manuscripts and the symbolic codes of the Old Masters, seems pertinent here: the Catholic Church as source of conspiracy is quite comfortably inconsequential when placed beside sensational media reports of contemporary terrors.

For Nicholas Royle, in his definitive work on *The Uncanny*, the destruction of the Twin Towers provided a powerful instance of the uncanny figuring itself in multiple ways:

> The appalling apparent accident of a plane flying into a skyscraper was followed minutes later by its uncanny repetition,

another plane crashing into the other skyscraper, immediately disconfirming (and yet still, in that moment, incredibly) any sense of the merely 'accidental'. As the twin towers collapsed, 'live' on television, and the images of this collapse were repeatedly screened over the hours that followed, a sense of the uncanny seemed all-pervading: Is this real? Is this really happening? Surely it's a film? Is this 'our' apocalypse now?[10]

Royle also notes the incidence of the uncanny in the telephone messages left by the dead; the coincidence that the date of the atrocity was also the number of the American emergency services; the 'blowback' (as it became popularly known) from past military and economic policies; the military training and support afforded bin Laden, the prime suspect, by the American government itself. While I would argue that the presence of the uncanny is not in itself confirmation of the Gothic, it is clear that since 9/11 the Western world's relationship with discourses that invoke terror must undergo some kind of alteration. Quite different examples of this can be provided by two productions released in 2005: the Hollywood film *Batman Begins*, directed by Christopher Nolan, and *Ghost Town*, a set of three novellas by Patrick McGrath.

Batman Begins was one of the more critically successful blockbusters of 2005, a kind of prequel to the loose sequence of films about the Gothically inflected comic-book hero. The links between Batman and the Gothic tradition have been repeatedly explored; while *Batman Begins* perhaps seemed less outwardly Gothic (and more of an action film) than Tim Burton's heavily stylized contributions to the series, *Batman* (1989) and *Batman Returns* (1992), the content of the film, with its reliance on notions of trauma, the return of the repressed, madness, secret organizations and underground spaces, drew heavily on Gothic convention. Although critical attention rested primarily on Christian Bale's performance as Batman, and the director Christopher Nolan's gritty sensibility, one of the most striking things about the film was its recycling of the contemporary mythology of terrorism. Bruce Wayne, it transpires, was trained by a secret organization hidden away in a camp somewhere in the mountains of eastern Asia, who operate according to fierce codes of honour and who are committed to wiping out the decadent capitalist culture represented by Gotham City. Bruce Wayne defects, rejecting their absolute moral codes, and they proceed to attack Gotham (long accepted as a fantasy version of New York) by releasing a chemical weapon that induces nightmarish hallucinations and – crucially – by running a subway train into the tallest building in the city, the Wayne Corporation, the ultimate symbol of capitalist empire-building. Released a few weeks prior to the London Tube bombings, this could not fail to be resonant.

What is interesting about *Batman Begins*, however, is that moral distinctions between the terrorists and the masked crusader who defeats them are repeatedly blurred. The mysterious members of the League of Shadows are initially shown as Bruce Wayne's saviours: they rescue him from a brutal Eastern prison and put him on the path to becoming a super-hero. Their desire to combat corruption and vice coincide with Bruce Wayne's own: it is only a difference of method and degree. In fact, Bruce Wayne's somewhat right-wing, vigilantist approach to crime is itself questioned as morally problematic by his love-interest, liberal lawyer Rachel Dawes. Moreover, in the repeated return to Bruce Wayne's childhood traumas, the death of his parents and his entrapment in a cave full of bats, Batman's heroism is shown to be profoundly troubling, rooted in psychic disorder and multiple returns of the repressed. The scene in which Wayne decides to rebuild his annihilated mansion exactly as it was before is reassuring – Batman has not been defeated – but also vaguely disturbing, contradicting any notion of emotional progress in the protagonist. This is a man who is so imprinted by his past that he is moved endlessly to recreate it. The film validates a rather reductive, popular Freudianism – Bruce Wayne dresses like a bat because he seeks to become what he fears – but it

Psychic returns and subterranean spaces: Christian Bale in Christopher Nolan's *Batman Begins* (2005).

does so in order to provide a far more complex moral vision than the standard Hollywood fare. Gothic discourses here provide not so much a medium for the expression of contemporary anxieties about terrorism (in fact it is questionable whether any adult who saw the film would be made genuinely anxious by it, it is so clearly figured as fantasy and as conforming with genre convention), but rather a means of raising questions about our Manichean divisions between good and bad, light and darkness, East and West, terrorists and vigilantes, in a popular, mainstream format.

In contrast, Patrick McGrath's *Ghost Town: Tales of Manhattan Then and Now*, an addition to the acclaimed Bloomsbury 'The Writer and the City' series, offers an explicit and 'high' cultural meditation on 9/11. The set of novellas provides a particularly vivid illustration both of how Gothic sensibilities have shifted and how they have stayed the same. McGrath's preceding seven novels and volumes of short stories all offered fresh reworkings of the familiar Gothic themes of 'transgression and decay', as he has characterized them.[11] *Ghost Town* continues to elaborate on these themes, but unifies them with a vivid evocation of the city of New York, which conjures up the unquiet ghosts not only of Ground Zero (the title of the third novella), but of the whole of the city's turbulent history.

Beginning with the American Revolution in 'The Year of the Gibbet', McGrath depicts the city in 1777 as a war zone occupied by British soldiers, one that cannot help recalling, on an oblique level, news images of contemporary Iraq. America, McGrath reminds us, was founded on acts of terrorism justified by an anti-imperialist ideology. At the same time, the opening sentence could describe the city post-9/11: 'I have been in the town, a disquieting experience, for New York has become a place not so much of death as of the *terror* of death.'[12] It is swiftly revealed, however, that this is 1832, and the city's decimation a result of cholera. The book is full of echoes across the centuries, as if the pain and suffering of the city are etched into the landscape; as if the city is a palimpsest of ruin and loss, haunted by ghosts of itself. The narrator of 'Ground Zero' compares the ruined towers to the skewed gravestones of Trinity Church, recalling 'the wreckage of some vast modernist cathedral'.[13] In doing so she unconsciously recalls the first narrator's description of the burning of Trinity, 'blazing like a fired ship . . . with a great crash the roof fell in and moments later the steeple came down after it in a fountain of fire'.[14] The two scenes of devastation occupy virtually the same site, their destruction figured as an uncanny repetition of trauma through history.

Critical discussions of American Gothic have frequently characterized it as exploring the dark side of the American dream of liberty and transcendence; for Leslie Fiedler, American literature *is* Gothic literature.[15] McGrath, although a British author, is clearly writing within this tradition: his text is fractured by a profound ambivalence. The dying narrator of 'The Year of the Gibbet' considers that

> Lately, in moments of nocturnal sentiment, in the back of some South Street grog shop, and disguised in liquor, I can still regard the Revolution as a struggle in which the cause prevailed because our destiny demanded that it do so; our *destiny*, yes. Though in the chill light of dawn that follows my illusions fade like a mist off the harbor and I remember a quite different narrative, one far darker.[16]

McGrath's narrator fiercely embodies the pride of New York in his refusal to leave his city for war or for disease, but this is undercut by his sense of personal guilt and failure, the reappearance of his mother's ghost and the decay of a city infected by creeping pestilence. In 'Ground Zero', the narrator reflects on President Bush's signing of the Patriot Act and the erosion of the Bill of Rights, acknowledging that once she would have been disturbed by this, but 'Not now. Not after what I've seen.'[17] The American rhetoric of liberty and independence is placed under threat throughout the text, the ghost of the mother who is hung for treason in front of her children in the first story a lingering spectral presence: at what price freedom? Despite the fulfilment of his mother's dreams – America is victorious, and established as an independent nation – the narrator of 'The Year of the Gibbet', and by extension the city, remains haunted.

This ambivalence is reconfigured in the second story, 'Julius', in which Noah van Horn, a flourishing nineteenth-century businessman, representative of the city's astonishing economic success, destroys his family by preventing the marriage of his son Julius to an Irish immigrant girl of uncertain virtue. The burgeoning metropolis is contrasted with the landscapes painted by Jerome Brook Franklin, a transcendentalist who believes that 'the true spirit of America lay in the vast sublimities of her boundless unspoiled wilderness'.[18] Yet the Catskill Mountains are presented as somewhat homely and benign – they are the location of the benevolent lunatic asylum where Julius van Horn is encouraged to paint landscapes in oils as a form of therapy – while the city itself takes on the qualities of the wilderness. Max Rinder, van Horn's protégée and eventual son-in-law, 'regarded the city as a lawless territory where ferocity, speed and cunning counted most: a state of nature'.[19] The American right to free enterprise is not the making of the van Horn family but its ultimate destruction, as Rinder buys the disappearance of Annie Kelly, triggering Julius's madness. The family tableau towards the end of the novel, in which 'a syphilitic robber-baron . . . a one-eyed painter and a man just out of an insane asylum' are linked together by the wordless bond between the three van Horn sisters, signals the corruption and decay that accompany the rapaciousness of capitalism.[20] The narrator Alice, Van Horn's great-grandchild, is left like the remnant of one of Hawthorne's family dynasties, pondering the family portraits and reflecting on the sins of the fathers, the harm done by prejudice and the devastating effects of repression:

> I understood that mine was not the only family in which violence
> and insanity had erupted in generations past, and plagued the

lives of those to come . . . it was Noah who denied Julius his chance of love, and why? Because of a prejudice acquired as a function of fear. Love must never be denied, never![21]

Alice's outburst acts as a kind of warning for contemporary Americans, albeit undercut by the hint at hidden tragedies in her own life story, inflecting her interpretation of the family narrative.

In McGrath's work, Gothic provides a language with which to discuss the pain and suffering caused by 9/11: a language of haunting, of guilt, of mental instability, of dereliction. The unreliable narrator of 'Ground Zero', a psychiatrist clearly far too invested in her client, is unsympathetic and lacking in self-awareness in the manner of an Edgar Allan Poe protagonist. Her emotional imbalance and dislocation, however, are hooked onto a real historical trauma; her personal inability to find closure in her professional relationship with Dan is echoed by that of the victims' relatives: 'I wonder about the woman from Battery Park, the one who wanted a funeral for her husband but had no body to put in the coffin. I would like to know if he got her a funeral. Did she find closure? Did she, Dan?'[22] Overall, McGrath's narrative recalls all kinds of earlier Gothic narratives, but these are put into the service of evoking an event that is absolutely historically and geographically specific.

Avery Gordon has suggested that: 'the ghost imports a charged strangeness into the place or sphere it is haunting, thus unsettling the propriety and property lines that delimit a zone of activity or knowledge'.[23] Ghosts, she suggests, are 'social figures', constructed by and through social relations. In *Ghost Town* the zone of activity that is unsettled is not only New York but America as a whole, the zone of knowledge the self-knowledge of a nation. For McGrath, haunting enables social critique that is also a kind of memorial to the dead. There can be no greater argument for Gothic's continued relevance.

References

Introduction: Reviving Gothic

1 Marquis de Sade, 'Extracts from "Ideé sur les romans"', trans. Victor Sage in *The Gothick Novel: A Casebook*, ed. Victor Sage (Basingstoke, 1990), p. 49.
2 Victor Sage and Allan Lloyd-Smith, eds, *Modern Gothic: A Reader* (Manchester, 1996), p. 4.
3 Chris Baldick, 'Introduction', in *The Oxford Book of Gothic Tales*, ed. C. Baldick (Oxford, 1992), pp. xi–xxiii (p. xiii).
4 David Punter, *The Literature of Terror: A History of Gothic Fictions from 1765 to the Present Day* (London, 1996).
5 Baldick, *Oxford Book of Gothic Tales*, p. xix.
6 Emily Dickinson, 'No. 670', in *The Complete Poems*, ed. Thomas H. Johnson (London, 1975), p. 333.
7 Robert Miles, *Gothic Writing, 1750–1820: A Genealogy* (London and New York, 1993).
8 Chris Baldick and Robert Mighall, 'Gothic Criticism', in *A Companion to the Gothic*, ed. David Punter (Oxford, 2000), pp. 209–28 (p. 227).
9 Ibid., p. 226.
10 Mark Edmundson, *Nightmare on Main Street: Angels, Sadomasochism and the Gothic* (Cambridge, MA, 1997).
11 Angela Carter, *Burning Your Boats: Collected Short Stories* (London, 1995), p. 460.
12 David Punter, 'Introduction: Of Apparitions', in *Spectral Readings: Towards a Gothic Geography*, ed. Glennis Byron and David Punter (Basingstoke, 1999), pp. 1–10 (p. 2).
13 Marquis de Sade, 'Extracts from "Ideé sur les romans"', p. 49.

14 Elaine Showalter, *Sexual Anarchy: Gender and Culture at the Fin-de-Siècle* (London, 1992); Robert Louis Stevenson, *The Strange Case of Dr Jekyll and Mr Hyde and Other Stories* (London, 1992), p. 109.

15 Christoph Grunenberg, 'Unsolved Mysteries: Gothic Tales from *Frankenstein* to the Hair-Eating Doll', in *Gothic: Transmutations of Horror in Late Twentieth-Century Art*, ed. Christoph Grunenberg (Boston, MA, 1997), pp. 212–160 (the pagination runs backwards in this volume).

16 E. J. Clery, *The Rise of Supernatural Fiction, 1762–1800* (Cambridge, 1995).

17 Alastair Fowler, *Kinds of Literature: An Introduction to the Theory of Genres and Modes* (Oxford, 1982), p. 109.

18 Jacques Derrida, 'The Law of Genre', trans. Avital Ronell, *Glyph 7* (1980), pp. 202–29.

19 Eve Kosofsky Sedgwick, *The Coherence of Gothic Conventions*, revd edn (London, 1986).

20 Allan Lloyd-Smith, 'Postmodernism / Gothicism', in *Modern Gothic: A Reader*, ed. Sage and Lloyd-Smith, pp. 6–19 (pp. 6, 8).

One: Mock Gothic

1 Jerrold Hogle, 'The Gothic Ghost of the Counterfeit and the Progress of Abjection', in *A Companion to the Gothic*, ed. David Punter (Oxford, 2000), pp. 293–304 (p. 298).

2 Ibid. See also Jean Baudrillard, *Simulations*, trans. Paul Foss, Paul Patton and Philip Beitchman (New York, 1983), p. 83.

3 Hogle, 'The Gothic Ghost of the Counterfeit', p. 300, quoting Bram Stoker, *Dracula*, ed. Maurice Hindle (London, 1993), pp. 31, 486.

4 Allan Lloyd-Smith, *American Gothic Fiction* (London and New York, 2004), p. 126.

5 Ibid.

6 E. J. Clery, *The Rise of Supernatural Fiction, 1762–1800* (Cambridge, 1995), p. 76.

7 Baudrillard, *Simulations*, p. 25.

8 Avril Horner and Sue Zlosnik, *Gothic and the Comic Turn* (Basingstoke, 2005), p. 4.

9 Ibid., p. 9.

10 Ann Radcliffe, 'On the Supernatural in Poetry', in *Gothic Documents: A Sourcebook, 1700–1820*, ed. E. J. Clery and Robert Miles (Manchester, 2000), pp. 163–72.

11 Mark Z. Danielewski, *House of Leaves* (London, 2001), p. ix.

12 Ibid., p. 512.

13 Ibid., p. 513.

14 Ibid., p. 514.

15 Charles Baudelaire, 'Les Fleurs du mal: Préface', in *Selected Poems*, trans. Joanna Richardson (Harmondsworth, 1986), p. 28.

16 Danielewski, *House of Leaves*, p. 514.

17 Ibid., p. xxiii.
18 J. G. Ballard, 'The Killer Inside', *The Guardian Film and Music* (23 September 2005), p. 5.
19 Danielewski, *House of Leaves*, p. 464.
20 Lloyd-Smith, *American Gothic Fiction*, p. 93.
21 Brian McHale, *Postmodernist Fiction* (London and New York, 1987), p. 50.
22 Elizabeth Gaskell, 'Disappearances', in *Gothic Tales*, ed. Laura Kranzler (Harmondsworth, 2000), pp. 1–10 (p. 10).
23 Rick Moody, 'On Gregory Crewdson', in *Twilight*, photographs by Gregory Crewdson (New York, 2002), pp. 6–11 (p. 6). Italics in the original.
24 Ken Gelder, *Reading the Vampire* (London and New York, 1994), p. 86.
25 Fredric Jameson, *Postmodernism; or, The Cultural Logic of Late Capitalism* (London and New York, 1991).
26 Eric Rhode, *A History of the Cinema from its Origins to 1970* (London, 1976), p. 183.
27 Derek Gregory, *Geographical Imaginations* (Oxford, 1994), p. 7.
28 Baudrillard, *Simulations*, p. 158 n. 8.
29 Ibid., p. 146.
30 Jerrold Hogle, 'The Gothic at our Turn of the Century: Our Culture of Simulation and the Return of the Body', in *The Gothic*, ed. Fred Botting (Cambridge, 2001), pp. 153–79 (pp. 160–61).

Two: Grotesque Bodies

1 *The Anatomists 3: A Modern Frankenstein*, broadcast Channel 4, 26 March 2002.
2 Fred Botting, 'Future Horror (The Redundancy of Gothic)', *Gothic Studies*, I/2 (December 1999), pp. 139–55 (p. 146).
3 Leslie Fiedler, *Freaks: Myths and Images of the Secret Self* (New York, 1978).
4 Mary Russo, *The Female Grotesque: Risk, Excess and Modernity* (London and New York, 1994), p. 62.
5 Mikhail Bakhtin, *Rabelais and His World*, trans. Helen Iswolsky (Bloomington, IN, 1984), p. 27.
6 Chris Baldick and Robert Mighall, 'Gothic Criticism', in *A Companion to the Gothic*, ed. David Punter (Oxford, 2000).
7 Bakhtin, *Rabelais and His World*, p. 37.
8 Ibid., p. 38.
9 Avril Horner and Sue Zlosnik, *Gothic and the Comic Turn* (Basingstoke, 2005), p. 17.
10 Chris Baldick, *In Frankenstein's Shadow: Myth, Monstrosity and Nineteenth-century Writing* (Oxford, 1987); Fred Botting, *Making Monstrous: Frankenstein, Criticism, Theory* (Manchester, 1991).

11 Fred Botting, 'Metaphors and Monsters', *Journal for Cultural Research*, VII/4 (2003), pp. 339–65 (p. 361).
12 Katherine Dunn, *Geek Love* (London, 1989), pp. 52–3.
13 Elaine Showalter, *Sexual Anarchy: Gender and Culture at the Fin-de-Siècle* (London, 1992); see especially Chapter 10: 'The Way We Write Now: Syphilis and AIDS'.
14 Will Self, *Dorian* (London, 2003), p. 236.
15 Ibid., p. 265.
16 Ibid., p. 271.
17 Sigmund Freud, 'The Uncanny', in *The Penguin Freud Library, Volume 14: Art and Literature*, trans. James Strachey, ed. Albert Dickson (Harmondsworth, 1990), pp. 335–76 (pp. 340, 345).
18 Self, *Dorian*, p. 276.
19 Ibid., p. 271.
20 Ibid., p. 273.
21 Ibid., p. 278.
22 Graham Ward, *True Religion* (Oxford, 2003), p. ix.
23 Ibid., p. 130.
24 Victor Sage, *Horror Fiction in the Protestant Tradition* (Basingstoke, 1988).
25 Examples are too numerous to give a comprehensive list, but see, for example, Stephen D. Arata, 'The Occidental Tourist: *Dracula* and the Anxiety of Reverse Colonization', *Victorian Studies*, XXXIII/4 (1990), pp. 621–45; Ken Gelder, *Reading the Vampire* (London and New York, 1994); Judith Halberstam, *Skin Shows: Gothic Horror and the Technology of Monsters* (Durham, NC, and London, 1995); H. L. Malchow, *Gothic Images of Race in Nineteenth-century Britain* (Stanford, CA., 1996).
26 Horner and Zlosnik, *Gothic and the Comic Turn*, p. 1.
27 Patrick McGrath, *Blood and Water and Other Stories* (Harmondsworth, 1989), p. 16.
28 Ibid., p. 13.
29 Ibid.
30 Ibid., p. 15.
31 Ibid., p. 6.

Three: Teen Demons

1 Eve Kosofsky Sedgwick, *The Coherence of Gothic Conventions* (London, 1986).
2 Rob Latham, *Consuming Youth: Vampires, Cyborgs and the Culture of Consumption* (Chicago, 2002), p. 67.
3 Ellen Moers, *Literary Women* (London, 1978), p. 107.
4 Robert Kiely, *The Romantic Novel in England* (Boston, MA, 1972), p. 73.
5 Samuel Taylor Coleridge, 'Review of *The Monk*', *Critical Review*, XIX (1797), pp. 194–200 (p. 197).
6 Jane Austen, *Northanger Abbey, Lady Susan, The Watsons and Sanditon*, ed. John

Davie (Oxford, 1980), p. 3.

7 John Aikin and Anna Laetitia Aikin, 'On the Pleasure Derived from Objects of Terror; with Sir Bertrand, A Fragment', in *Gothic Documents: A Sourcebook, 1700–1820*, ed. E. J. Clery and Robert Miles (Manchester, 2000), pp. 127–32 (p. 129), first published in *Miscellaneous Pieces in Prose* (London, 1773), pp. 119–37.

8 Elizabeth Napier, *The Failure of the Gothic: Problems of Disjunction in an Eighteenth Century Literary Form* (Oxford, 1987), p. 147.

9 Chris Baldick, ed., *The Oxford Book of Gothic Tales* (Oxford, 1992), p. xiii.

10 Johnny Cigarettes and James Oldham, 'But for the Grace of Goth', *Vox* (August 1997), p. 65.

11 Ellen Barry, 'Still Gothic After All These Years', *Boston Phoenix* (31 July– 7 August 1997: http://www.bostonphoenix.com/archive/features/97/07/31/GOTH_2).

12 Dave Simpson, 'I Have Seen the Future – and It's Goth', *The Guardian* (21 March 2006: http://arts.guardian.co.uk/features/story/0,,1735690,00.html).

13 Dick Hebdige, *Subculture: The Meaning of Style* (London, 1979).

14 Eve Kosofsky Sedgwick, *The Coherence of Gothic Conventions*, revd edn (London, 1986).

15 Catherine Spooner, *Fashioning Gothic Bodies* (Manchester, 2004), p. 159.

16 Carol J. Clover, *Men, Women and Chainsaws: Gender in the Modern Horror Film* (London, 1992), p. 59.

17 Angela McRobbie and Jenny Garber, 'Girls and Subcultures', in *The Subcultures Reader*, ed. Ken Gelder and Sarah Thornton (New York, 1996), pp. 112–20.

18 Huggy Bear, 'Hopscortch', on . . . *Our Troubled Youth*, double-sided album with Bikini Kill, *Yeah, Yeah, Yeah, Yeah* (Catcall, 1993).

19 Diane Purkiss , *The Witch in History: Early Modern and Twentieth-century Representations* (London, 1996), p. 45.

20 *Teenage Kicks: The Witch Craze*, broadcast Channel 4, 27 August 2002.

21 Gregory A. Waller, 'Introduction to *American Horrors*', in *The Horror Reader*, ed. Ken Gelder (London, 2000), pp. 256–64 (p. 261).

22 David Punter, *The Literature of Terror: A History of Gothic Fictions from 1765 to the Present Day, Volume 2: The Modern Gothic* (London, 1996), p. 150.

23 Max Nordau, *Degeneration* (London, 1896).

24 Mark Beaumont, 'Marilyn Manson', *New Musical Express* (25 September 2004), p. 36.

25 Patricia Cornwell, *Portrait of a Killer: Jack the Ripper – Case Closed* (London, 2003).

26 Poppy Z. Brite, *Lost Souls* (Harmondsworth, 1994).

27 Katherine Ramsland, *Piercing the Darkness: Undercover with Vampires in America Today* (London, 1999), p. 204.

28 Ibid., p. 6.

29 Ibid., p. 104.

30 Ibid., pp. 144–5.

31 Lucy Ward, 'Send in Buffy To Save Lost Girls – Ofsted Chief', *The Guardian* (6 March 2004), p. 12. Ofsted stands for the Office for Standards in Education (England).

32 Justine Larbalestier, '*Buffy*'s Mary Sue is Jonathan: *Buffy* Acknowledges the Fans', in *Fighting the Forces: What's at Stake in Buffy the Vampire Slayer*, ed. Rhonda V. Wilcox and David Lavery (Lanham, MD, 2002).

33 Judith Butler, *Gender Trouble: Feminism and the Subversion of Identity* (London, 1990), p. 137.

34 Ibid., p. 141.

35 Marti Noxon interviewed on 'A Buffy Bestiary', *Buffy the Vampire Slayer Season Two DVD Collection* (2001). Early Goth overlapped significantly with the final death-throes of Punk, with bands later defined as Goth such as Siouxsie and the Banshees (who featured Sid Vicious in an early line-up) emerging from the Punk scene in the late 1970s.

36 Sarah Thornton, *Club Cultures: Music, Media and Subcultural Capital* (Cambridge, 1995).

Four: Gothic Shopping

1 David J. Skal, *Hollywood Gothic: The Tangled Web of 'Dracula' from Stage to Screen* (London, 1992), p. 195.

2 Rob Latham, *Consuming Youth: Vampires, Cyborgs and the Culture of Consumption* (Chicago, 2002), p. 25.

3 Ibid.

4 Chris Baldick, *In Frankenstein's Shadow: Myth, Monstrosity and Nineteenth-century Writing* (Oxford, 1990), pp. 127–8.

5 *Taste 1: Gothic*, broadcast BBC 2, January 2002.

6 Paul Hodkinson, *Goth: Identity, Style and Subculture* (Oxford, 2002).

7 Ted Polhemus, *Street Style: From Sidewalk to Catwalk* (London, 1994), pp. 97–9.

8 Caroline Evans, 'Yesterday's Emblems and Tomorrow's Commodities: The Return of the Repressed in Fashion Imagery Today', in *Fashion Cultures: Theories, Explorations and Analysis*, ed. Stella Bruzzi and Pamela Church Gibson (London and New York, 2000), pp. 93–113 (p. 106).

9 Ibid., p. 107.

10 Ibid.

11 Eve Kosofsky Sedgwick, *The Coherence of Gothic Conventions*, revd edn (London 1986).

12 Vance Packard, *The Hidden Persuaders* (London, 1957), pp. 8, 4.

13 Greg Myers, *Ad Worlds: Brands, Media, Audiences* (London, 1998).

14 Warren Berger, *Advertising Today* (London, 2001).

15 *100 Scariest Moments*, broadcast Channel 4, 26 October 2003.

16 Fred Botting, *Making Monstrous: Frankenstein, Criticism, Theory* (Manchester, 1991), pp. 192–3.

17 Ibid., p. 202.

18 The Sisters of Mercy, 'This Corrosion', on *Floodland* (Merciful Release, 1987), lyrics by Andrew Eldritch.

19 Angela McRobbie, *Postmodernism and Popular Culture* (London, 1994).
20 Henry Jenkins, *Textual Poachers: Television Fans and Participatory Culture* (London and New York, 1992).
21 Temporary posting at www.livingdeaddolls.com.
22 Hélène Cixous, 'Fiction and its Phantoms: A Reading of Freud's *Das Unheimliche*', *New Literary History*, VII/3 (1976), pp. 525–48.

Conclusion: The End of Gothic?

1 William Blake, *The Marriage of Heaven and Hell*, in *Complete Writings*, ed. Geoffrey Keynes (Oxford, 1966), pp. 148–58 (p. 150).
2 Fred Botting, 'Candygothic', in *The Gothic*, ed. Fred Botting (Cambridge, 2001), pp. 133–51 (p. 134).
3 Fred Botting, 'Aftergothic: Consumption, Machines and Black Holes', in *The Cambridge Companion to Gothic Fiction*, ed. Jerrold E. Hogle (Cambridge, 2002), pp. 277–300 (p. 298).
4 Ibid., p. 281.
5 Chris Baldick, ed., *The Oxford Book of Gothic Tales* (Oxford, 1992), p. xxii.
6 Edmund Burke, *Reflections on the Revolution in France*, ed. Conor Cruise O'Brien (Harmondsworth, 1986).
7 Ronald Paulson, *Representations of Revolution, 1789–1820* (New Haven, CT, 1983).
8 Johan Höglund, 'Gothic Haunting Empire', in *Memory, Haunting, Discourse*, ed. Maria Holmgren Troy and Elisaberh Wennö (Karlstad, 2005), pp. 233–44 (p. 241).
9 Baldick, *The Oxford Book of Gothic Tales*, p. xiii.
10 Nicholas Royle, *The Uncanny* (Manchester, 2003), pp. vii–vii.
11 Patrick McGrath, 'Transgression and Decay', in *Gothic: Transmutations of Horror in Late Twentieth Century Art*, ed. Christoph Grunenberg (Boston, MA, 1997), pp. 158–53 (the pagination runs backwards in this volume).
12 Patrick McGrath, *Ghost Town: Tales of Manhattan Then and Now* (London, 2005), p. 1.
13 Ibid., p. 195.
14 Ibid., pp. 13–14.
15 Leslie Fiedler, *Love and Death in the American Novel* (New York, 1966).
16 McGrath, *Ghost Town*, p. 4.
17 Ibid., p. 240.
18 Ibid., p. 75.
19 Ibid., p. 117.
20 Ibid., pp. 155–6.
21 Ibid., pp. 172–3.
22 Ibid., p. 243.
23 Avery Gordon, *Ghostly Matters: Haunting and the Sociological Imagination* (Minneapolis, MN, 1997), p. 63.

Acknowledgements

Special thanks are due to Emma McEvoy, my best and most indefatigable reader and critic. Thanks too to colleagues at Lancaster University who read and made invaluable comments on individual chapters: Arthur Bradley, Jo Carruthers, Mike Greaney, Lindsey Moore and Andy Tate. Fred Botting was particularly helpful in providing encouragement and ongoing debate, and Chris Baldick, Simon Eliot and Alison Findlay offered guidance at various stages. Crucially, however, this book has been shaped by discussion with students: at the beginning, members of my much-missed 'Gothic and Grotesque' seminars at University College Falmouth – specifically Arwen, Chrisy, Eileen, Jo, Lou, Margaret, Sian and Tina; and at the end, Jenny Collyer, and members of my MA seminars in 'Contemporary Gothic' at Lancaster University. Sharon Borthwick, Jo Harrop and Christina Warren were excellent partners in tracking down Gothic phenomena.

Thanks to Cathy de Monchaux and FRED, the Gagosian Gallery, Gregory Crewdson and Luhring Augustine, Jay Jopling and White Cube, Joel-Peter Witkin and Hasted Hunt Gallery, Mike Smith, Nick Knight and Aimee Mullins for generously granting permission to reproduce their work or that of the artists they represent.

I am grateful to Lancaster University's Faculty of Arts and Social Sciences' Research and Enterprise Fund for contributing to picture costs.

Thanks to Barrie Bullen for initially seeing the book's potential, and my editor Michael Leaman for being patient.

Finally, Eddie Robson has been an immeasurable source of support throughout – this book is for him.

List of Illustrations

p. 81: Patricia Arquette as Frankie in Rupert Wainwright's *Stigmata* (1999).

p. 84: Joel-Peter Witkin, *Las Meninas New Mexico*, 1987, toned gelatin silver print photograph. Museum of Fine Arts, Santa Fe, New Mexico. Photo: courtesy of the artist and Hasted Hunt Gallery, New York.

p. 88: The Gothic heroine: a woodcut from the 1832 edition of Ann Radcliffe's *The Romance of the Forest*.

p. 92: A contemporary interpretation of the Gothic heroine, at Whitby Gothic Weekend, April 2005. Photo: © Mike Smith 2005.

p. 93: Contemporary Goth, as seen at Whitby Gothic Weekend, in 2005. Photo: © Mike Smith 2005.

p. 95: Goth style icon Siouxsie Sioux, 1983. Photo: Rex Features/Eugene Adebari (103247A).

p. 96: The Dresden Dolls' Gothic-tinged 'Brechtian Punk Cabaret', 2006. Photo: Lisa Lunskayer Gordon/http://www. dresdendolls. com/

p. 97: Gothic Country: The Handsome Family, 2003. Photo: Ted Jurney/ http://www. handsomefamily. com/

p. 108: Marilyn Manson, 2005. Photo: Rex Features/Charles Sykes (521573CC).

p. 110: 'Satanic' killer Manuela Ruda in court, 2002. Photo: Rex Features/Action Press (375685D).

p. 121: Dark Willow does Goth power-dressing in Season Six of the TV show *Buffy the Vampire Slayer*, 2002.

p. 124: A still from Tod Browning's 1931 *Dracula* showing Bela Lugosi in the title role. Photo: Rex Features/SNAP (390881JI).

p. 128 (top): Contemporary Goth style at Whitby Gothic Weekend, April 2005. Photo: © Mike Smith 2005.

p. 128 (foot): Model Aimee Mullins in 'Access-Able', from *Dazed and Confused*, September, 1998. Photo: Nick Knight, courtesy of Nick Knight.

p. 129: Fashion itself as imprisoning agent of the Gothic in Alexander McQueen's show for London Fashion Week, 2001. Photo Rex Features/XPO (326601G).

p. 132: Angelina Jolie in Versace at the 2000 Academy Awards ceremony. Photo Rex Features/CSP (323037B).

p. 147: Living Dead Dolls exclusive set, 'Nosferatu and Victim', released 2003. Photo courtesy of the author.

p. 161: Christian Bale in Christopher Nolan's *Batman Begins* (2005). Photo: Rex Features/Warner Bro/Everett (511568BF).